Celtic Crosses for the Soul

including creative and powerful Celtic Crosses designs, inspired by Soul, Mind, Body and Heart.

Karthic Praveen

SAMPLE

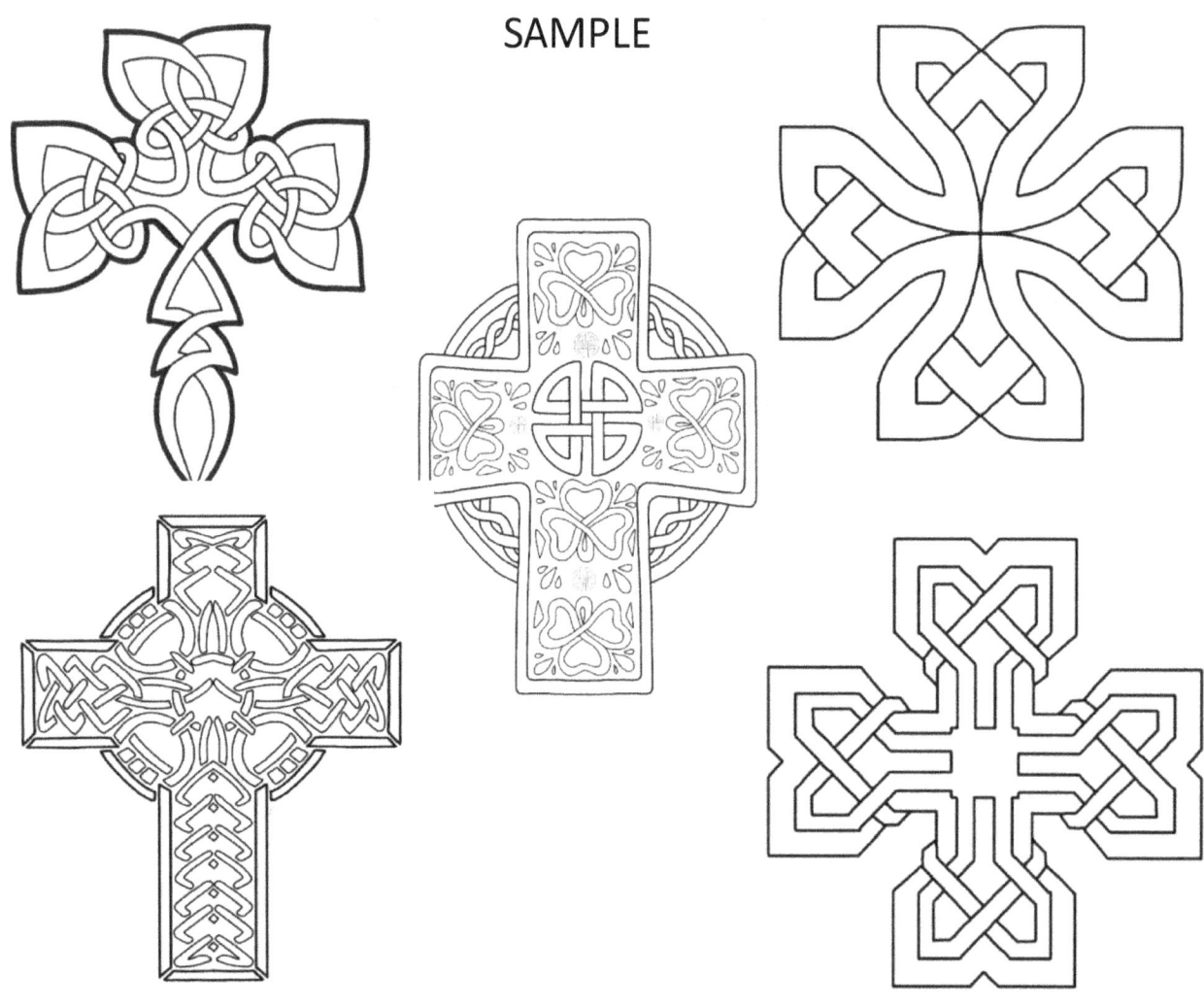

Introduction:

The Celtic Cross is a wonderful representation of faith and hope, represented with a circle around the intersection of the arms and stem evokes the strength, knowledge and compassion needed to handle life uncertainty.

the four arms of the Celtic Cross represent the four elements Fire, Air , Earth and Water also circle forms in Celtic Cross Symbolize God´s endless love.

Celtic Crosses for the Soul Coloring book includes different designs of Celtic Crosses that allow you to experience fulfillment and power, increasing your sense of faith and compassion throughout the creative process.

Inspire yourself!!

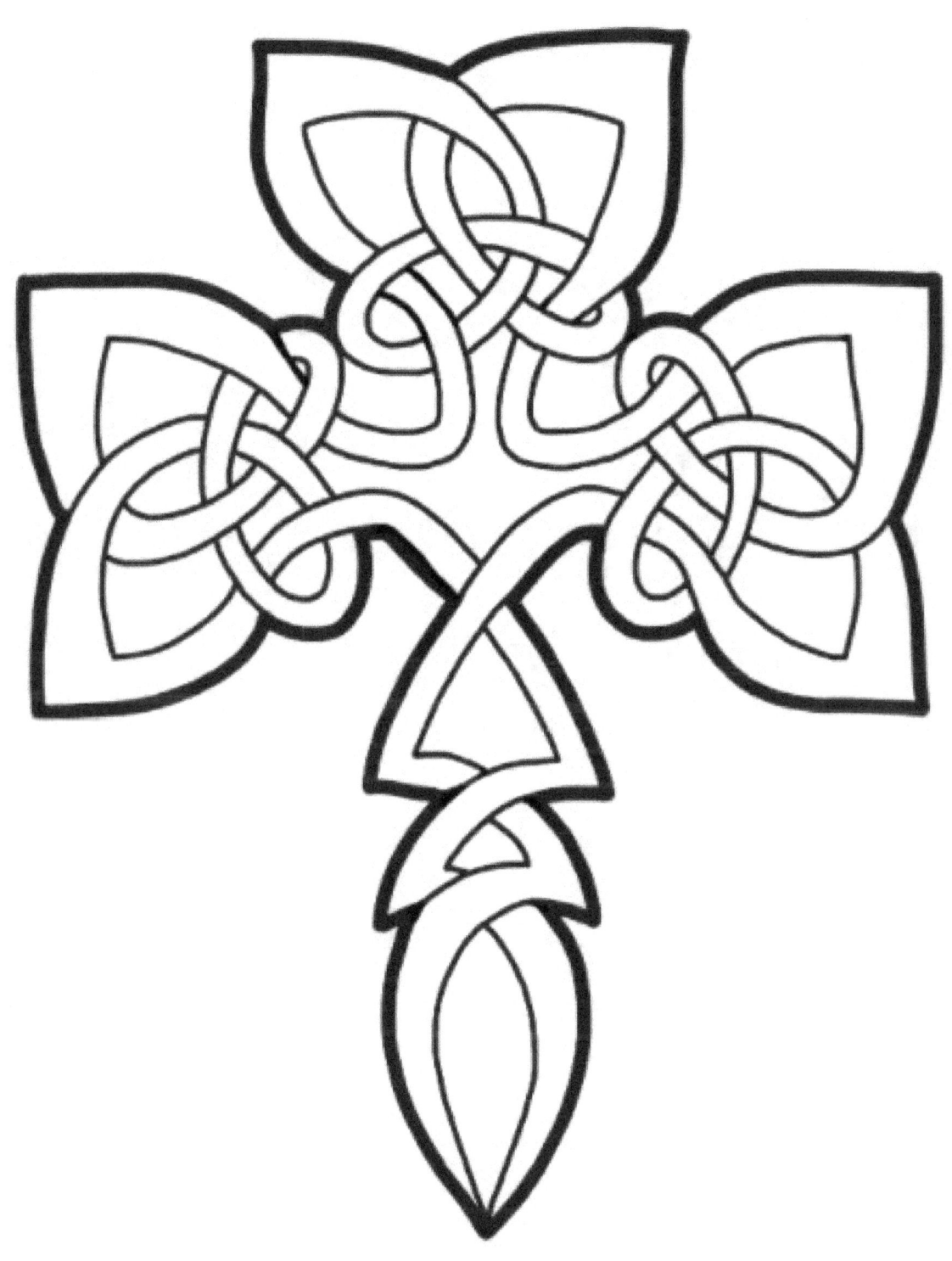

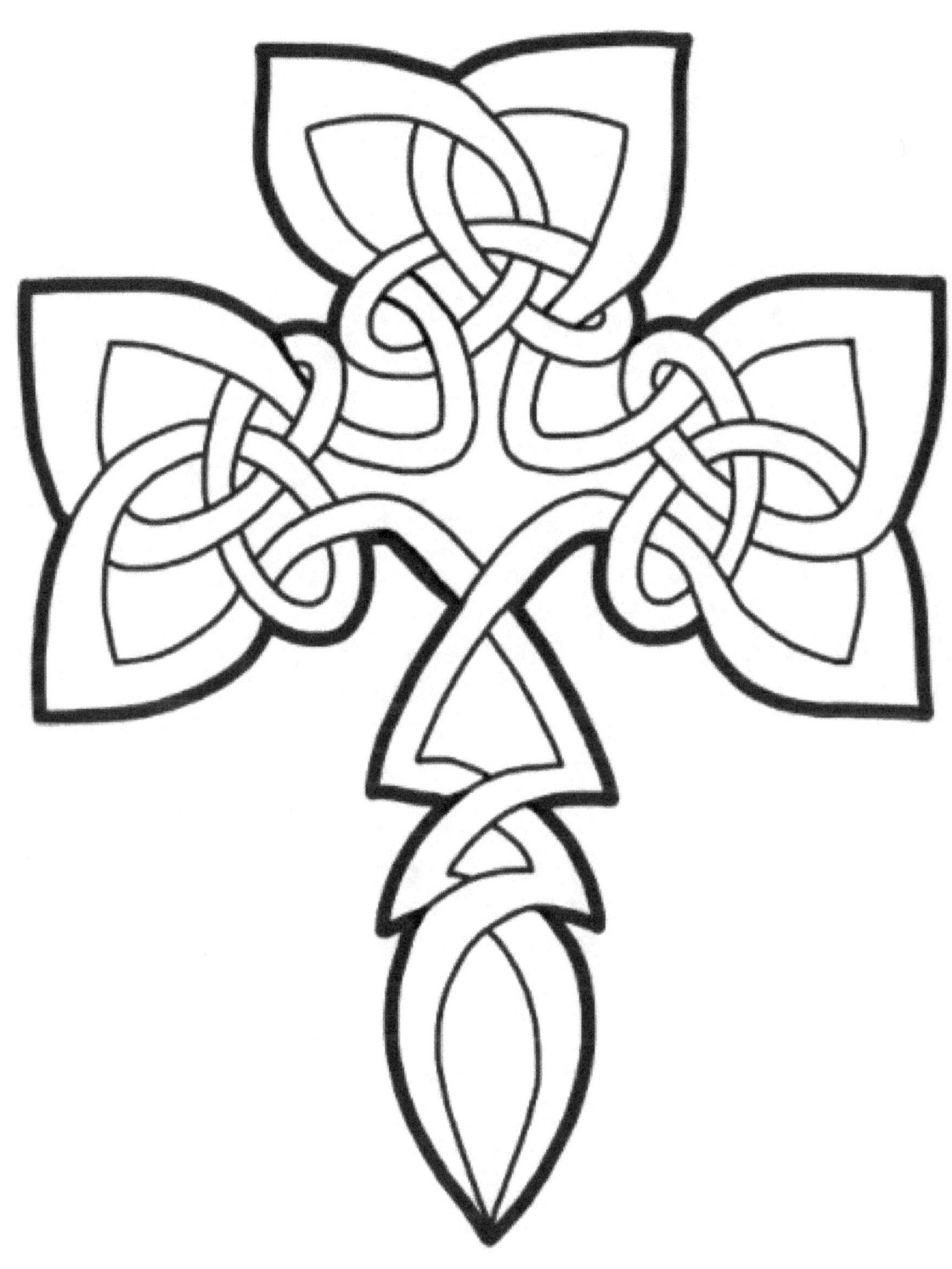

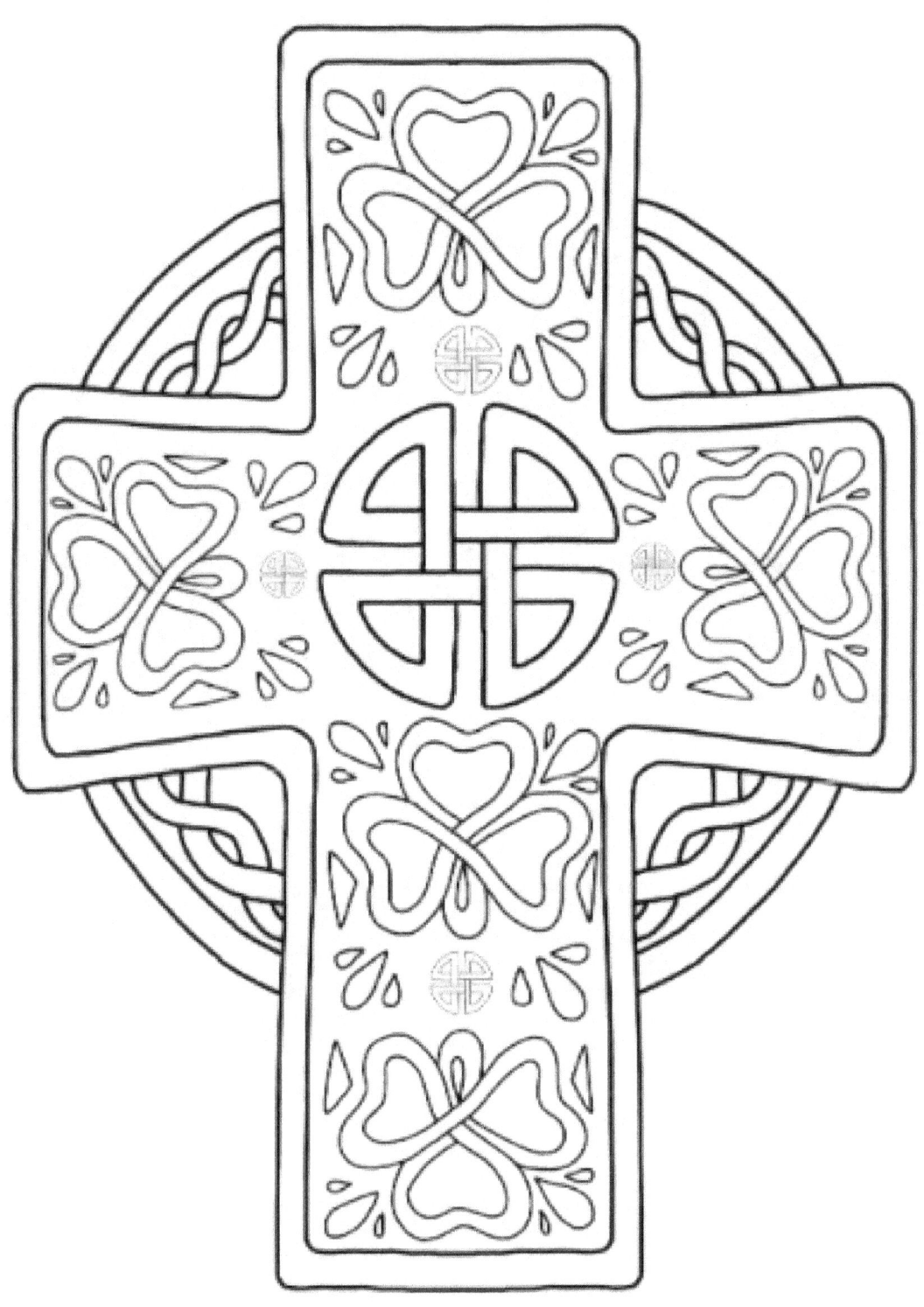

10

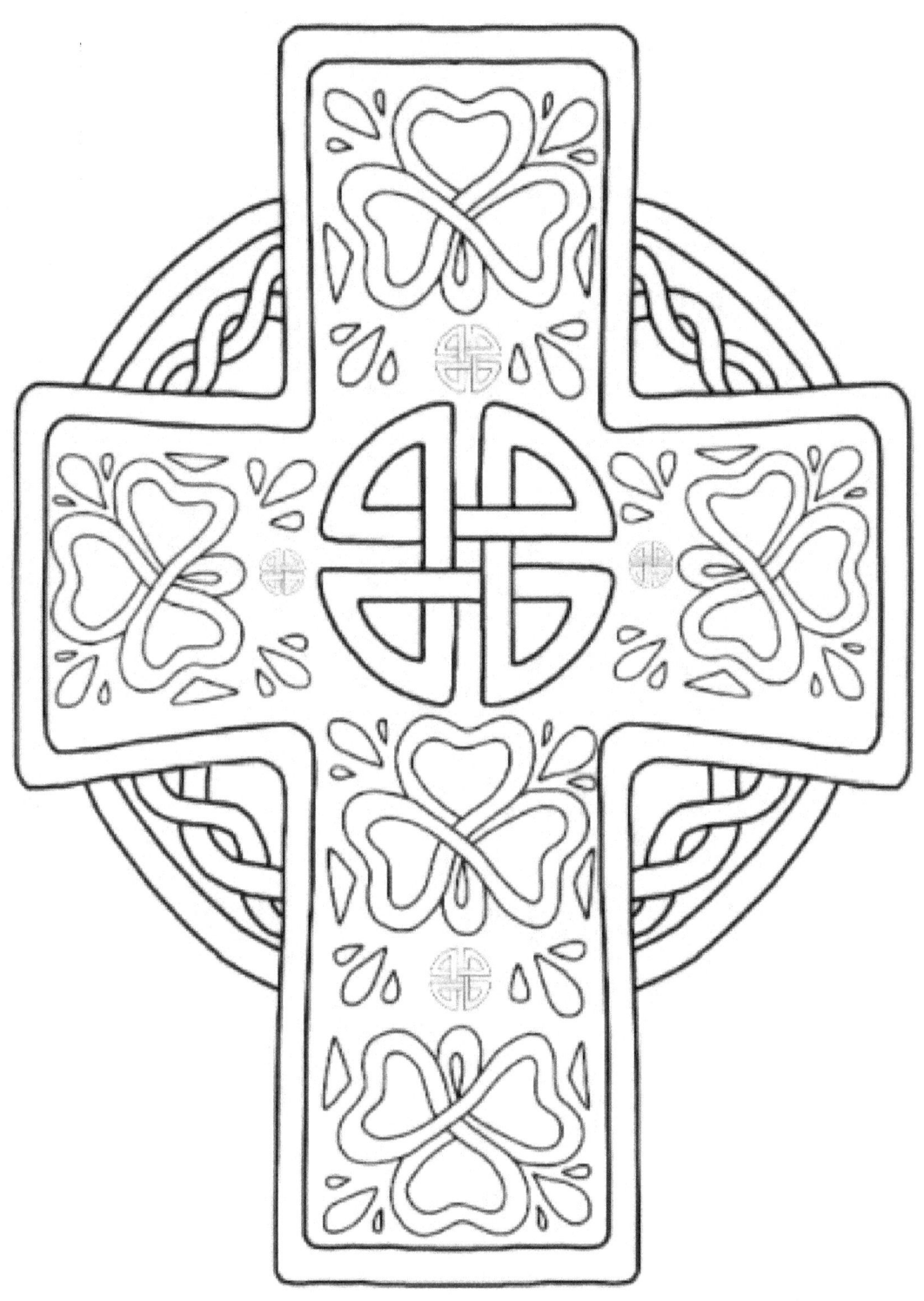

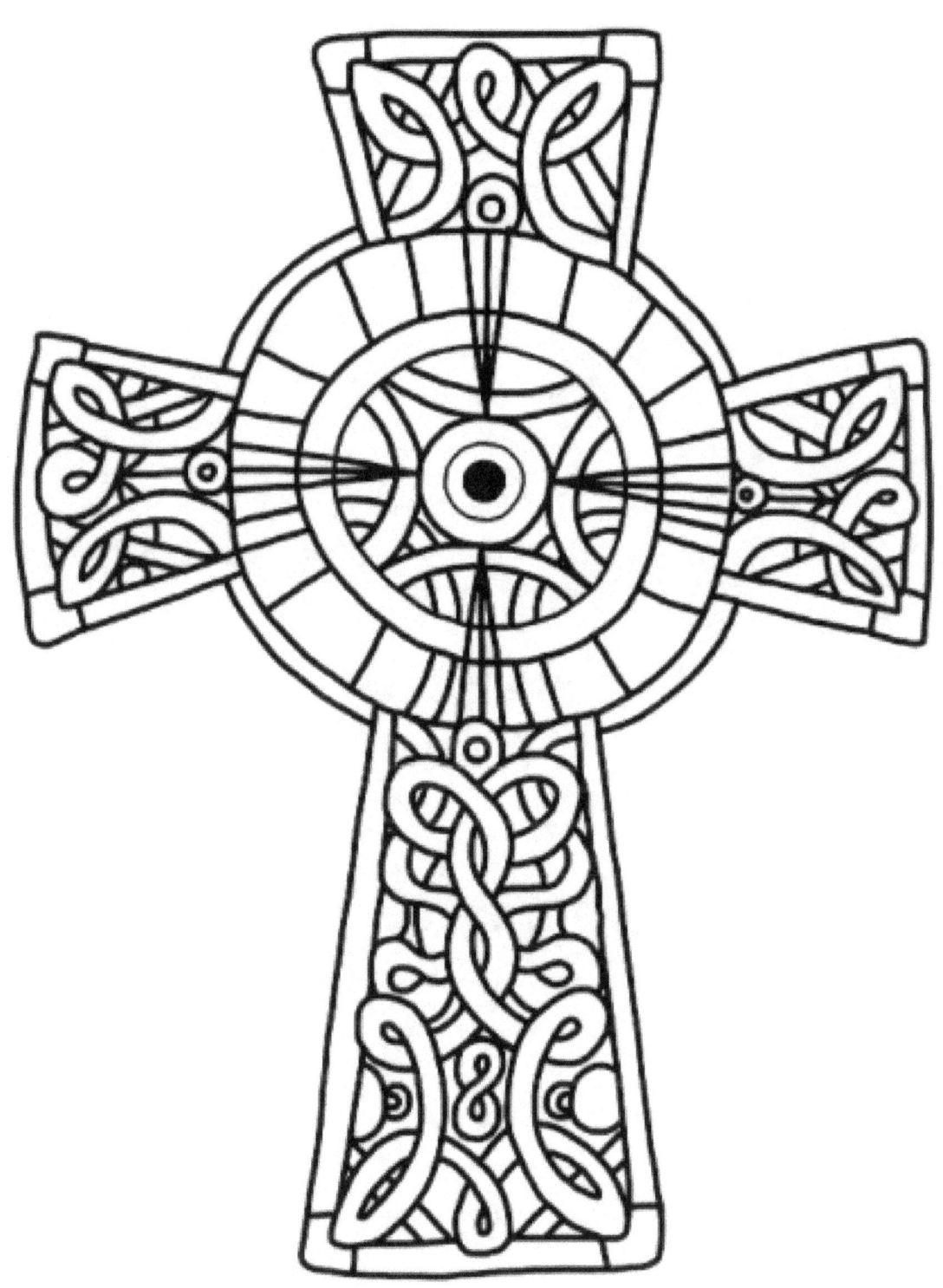

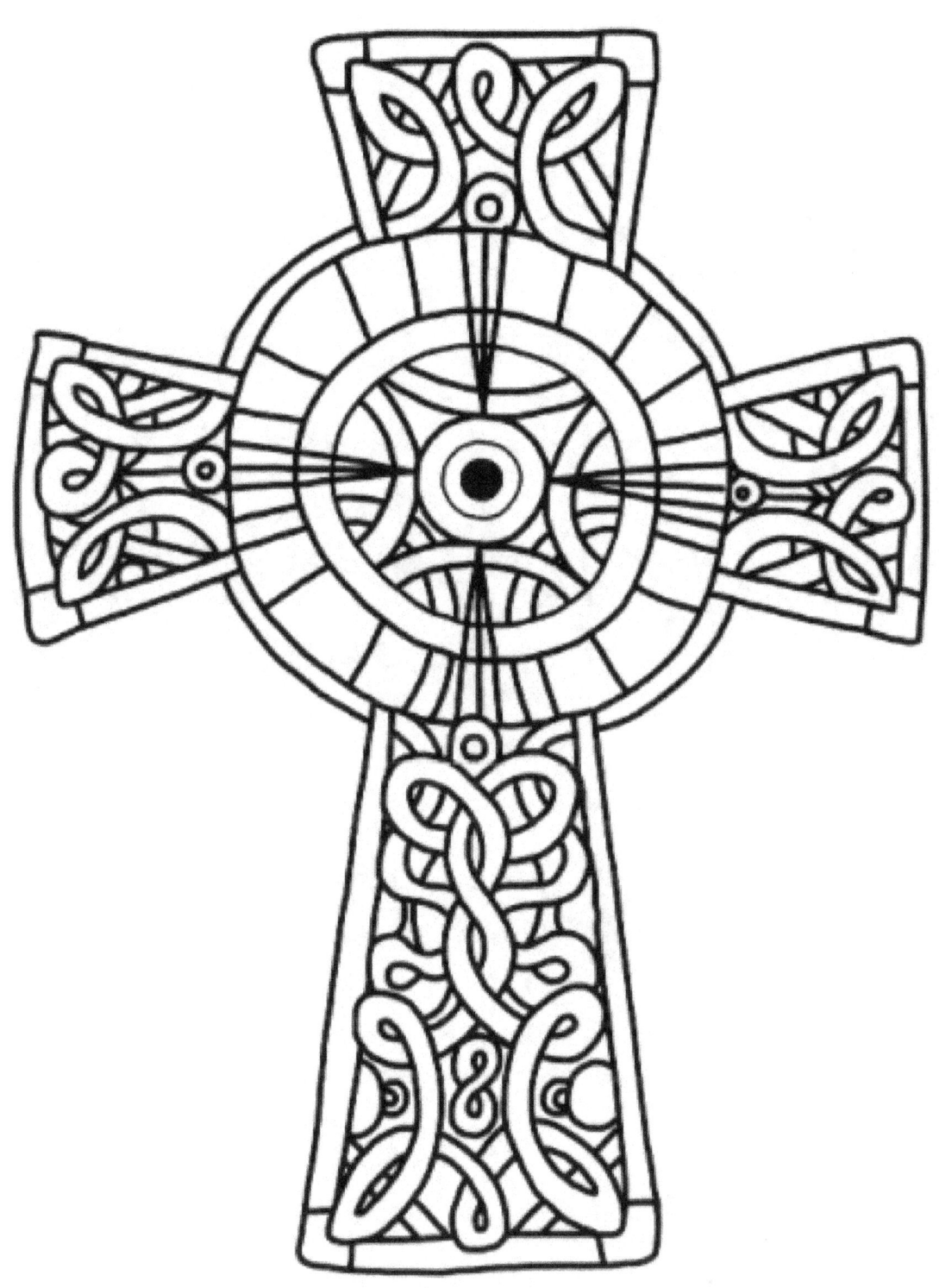

15

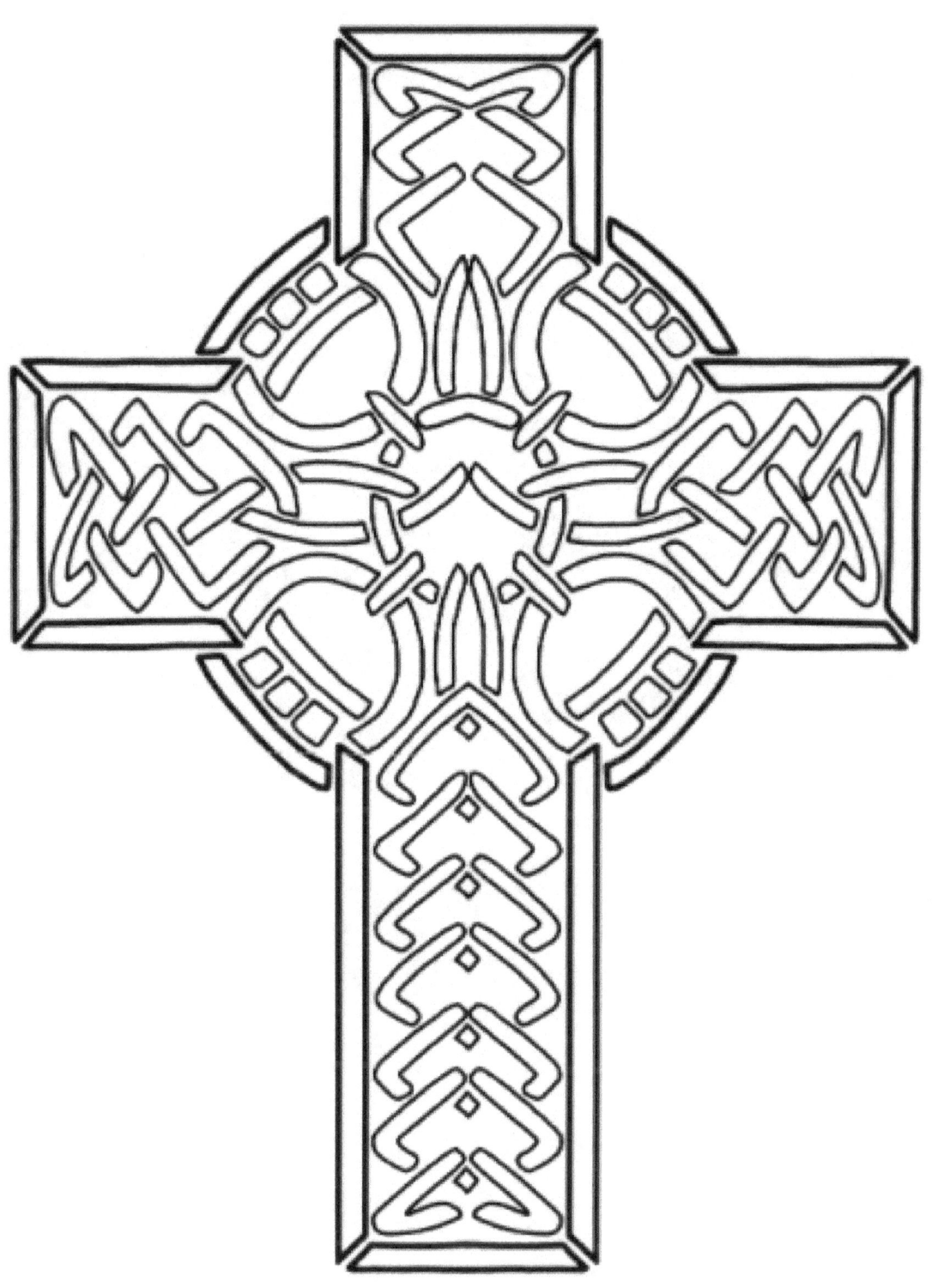

17

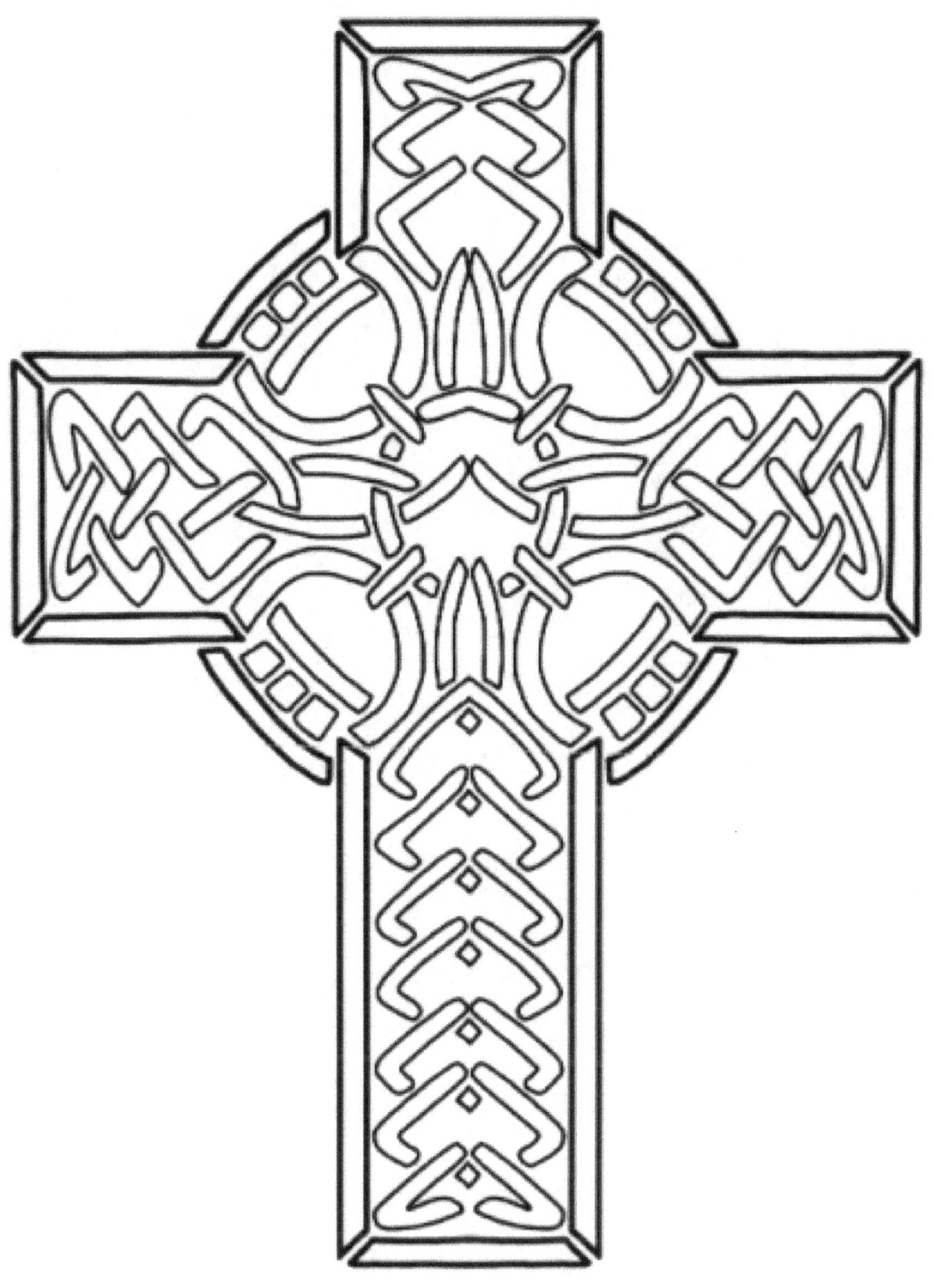

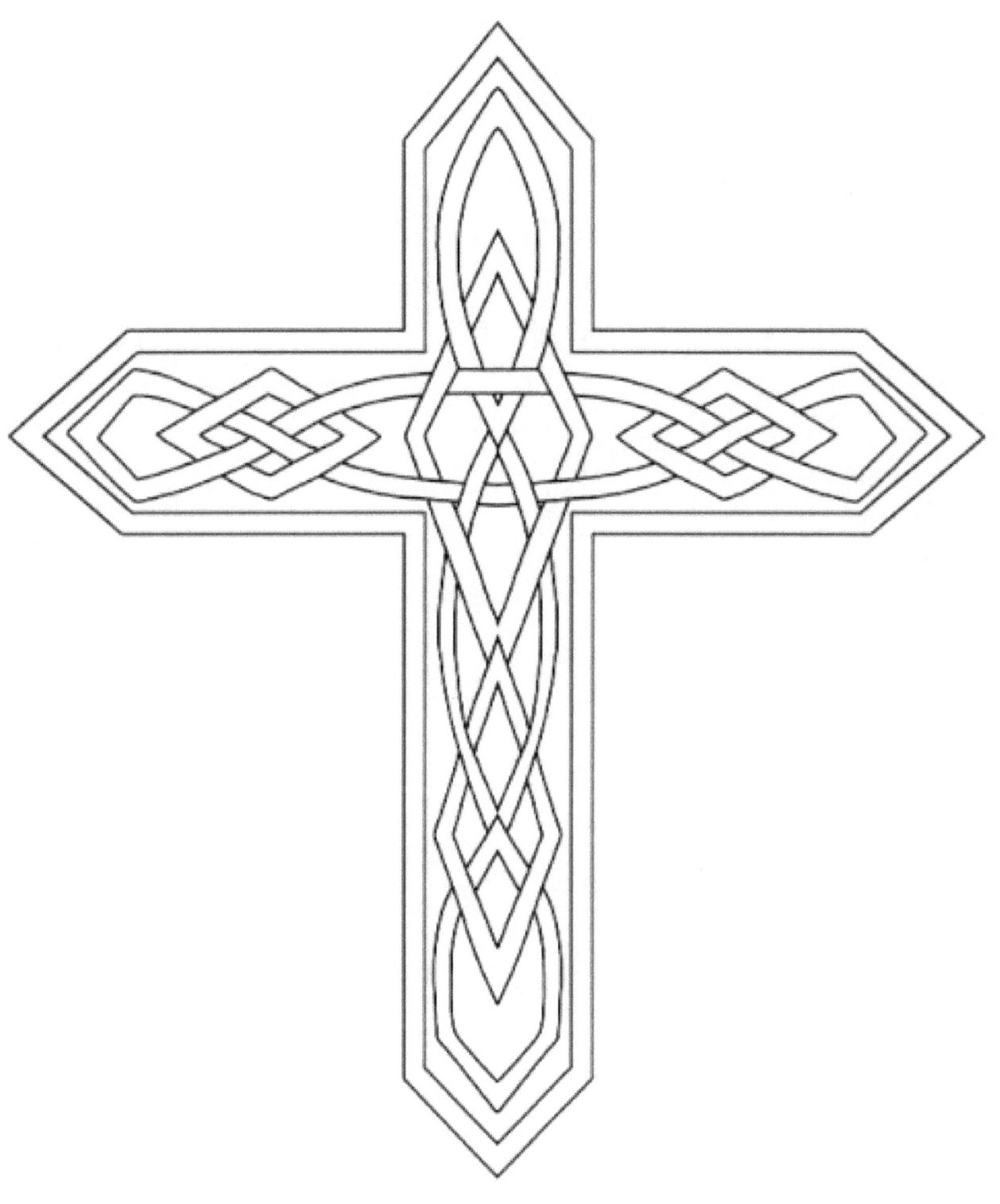

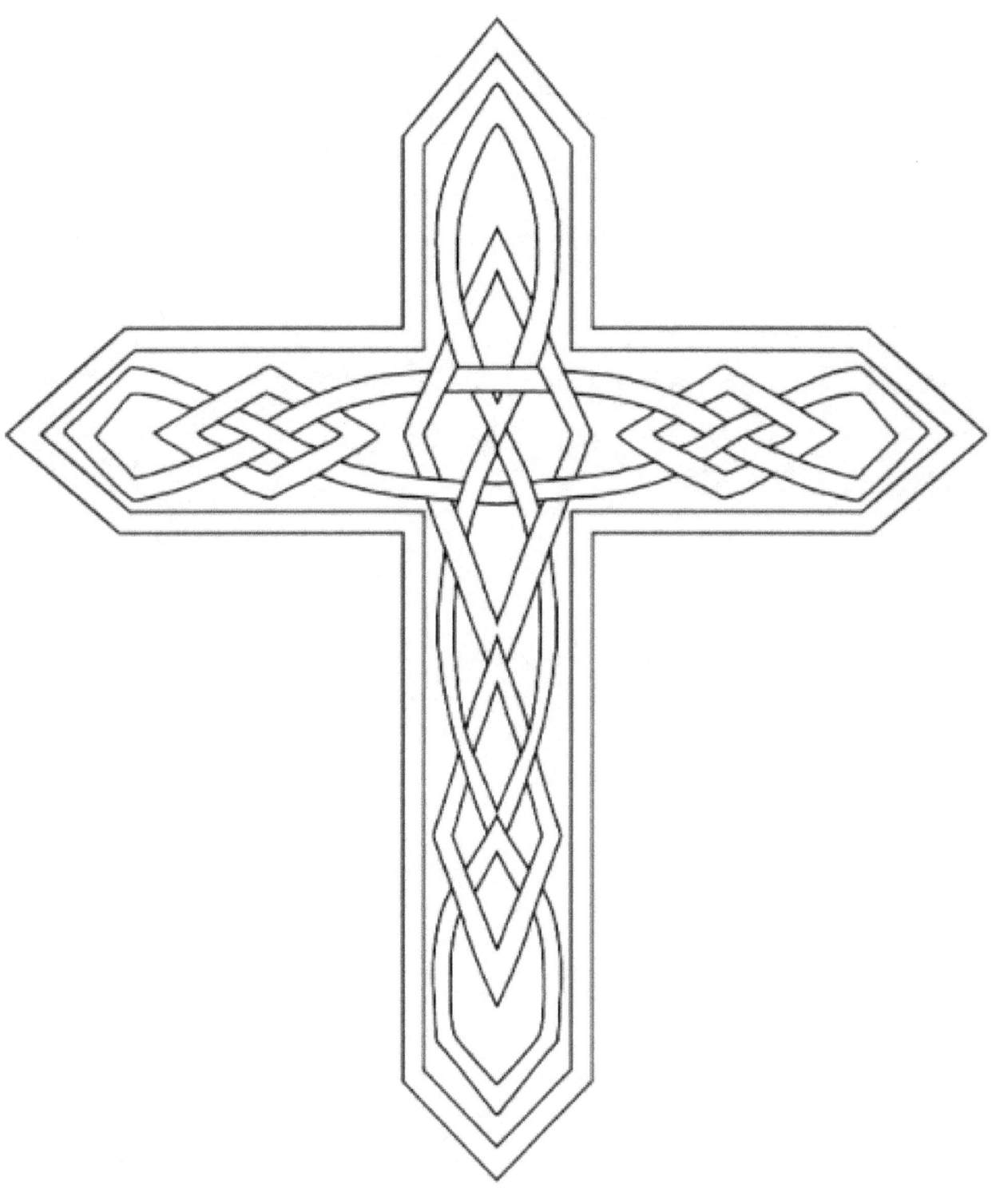

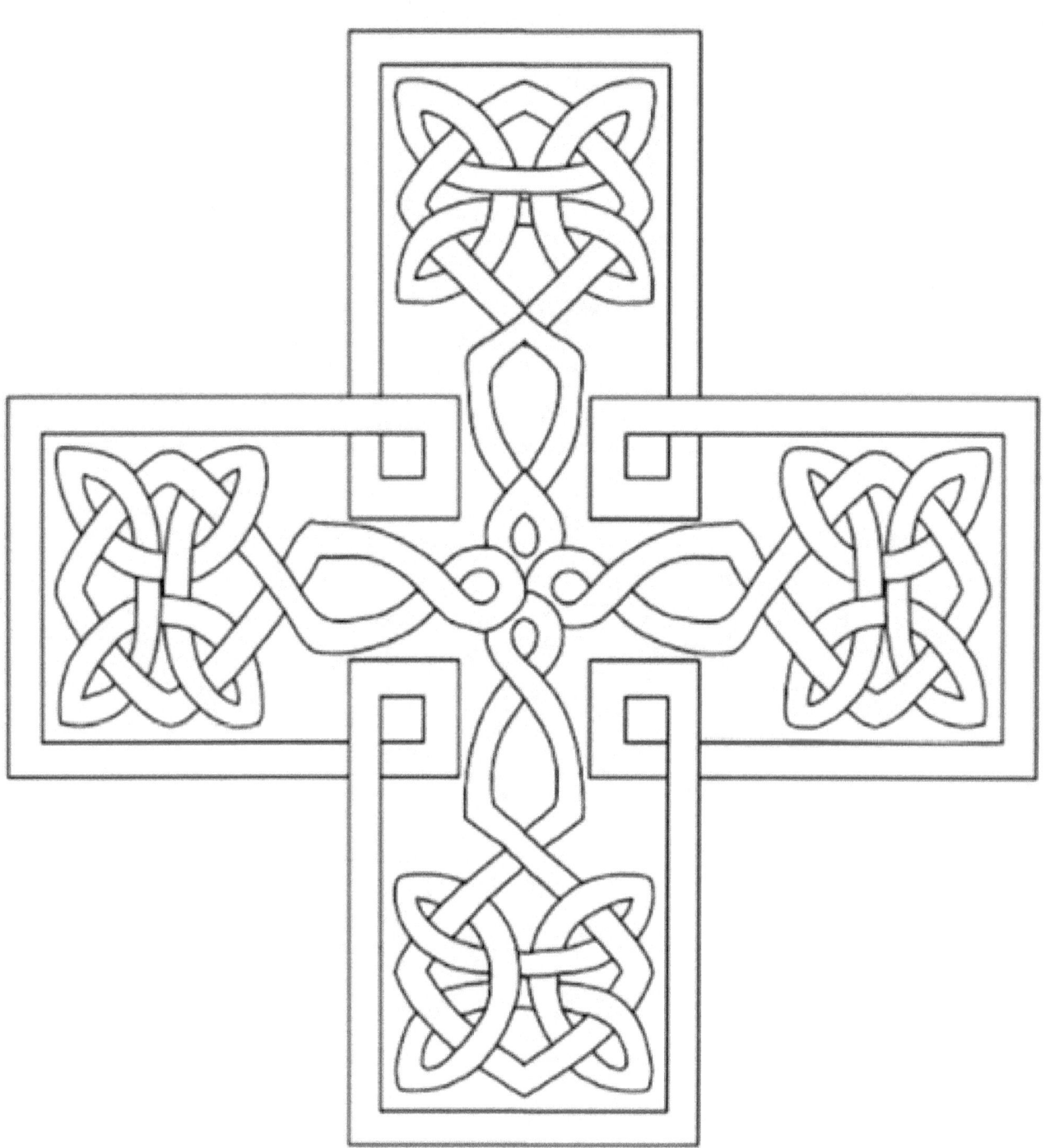

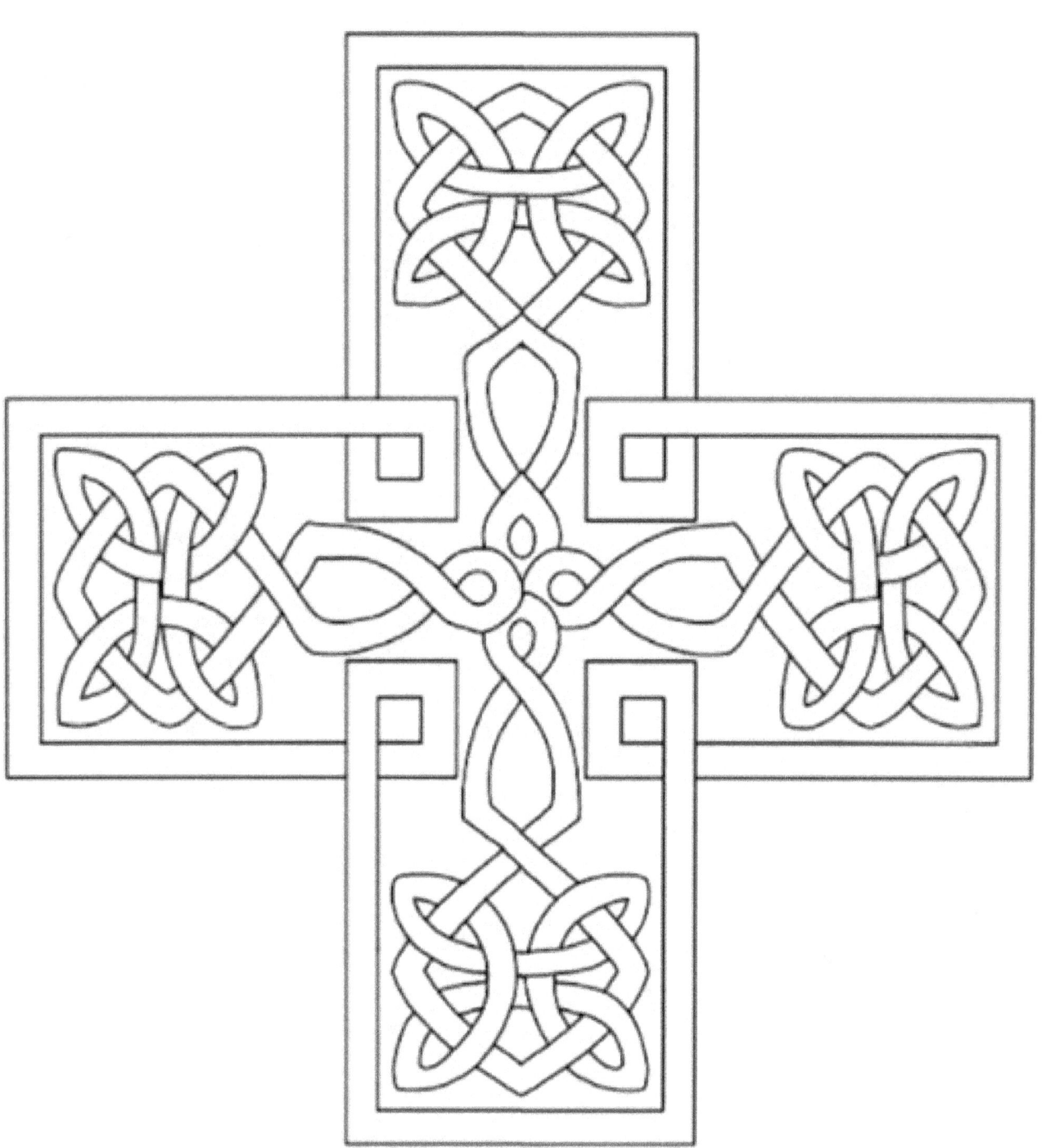

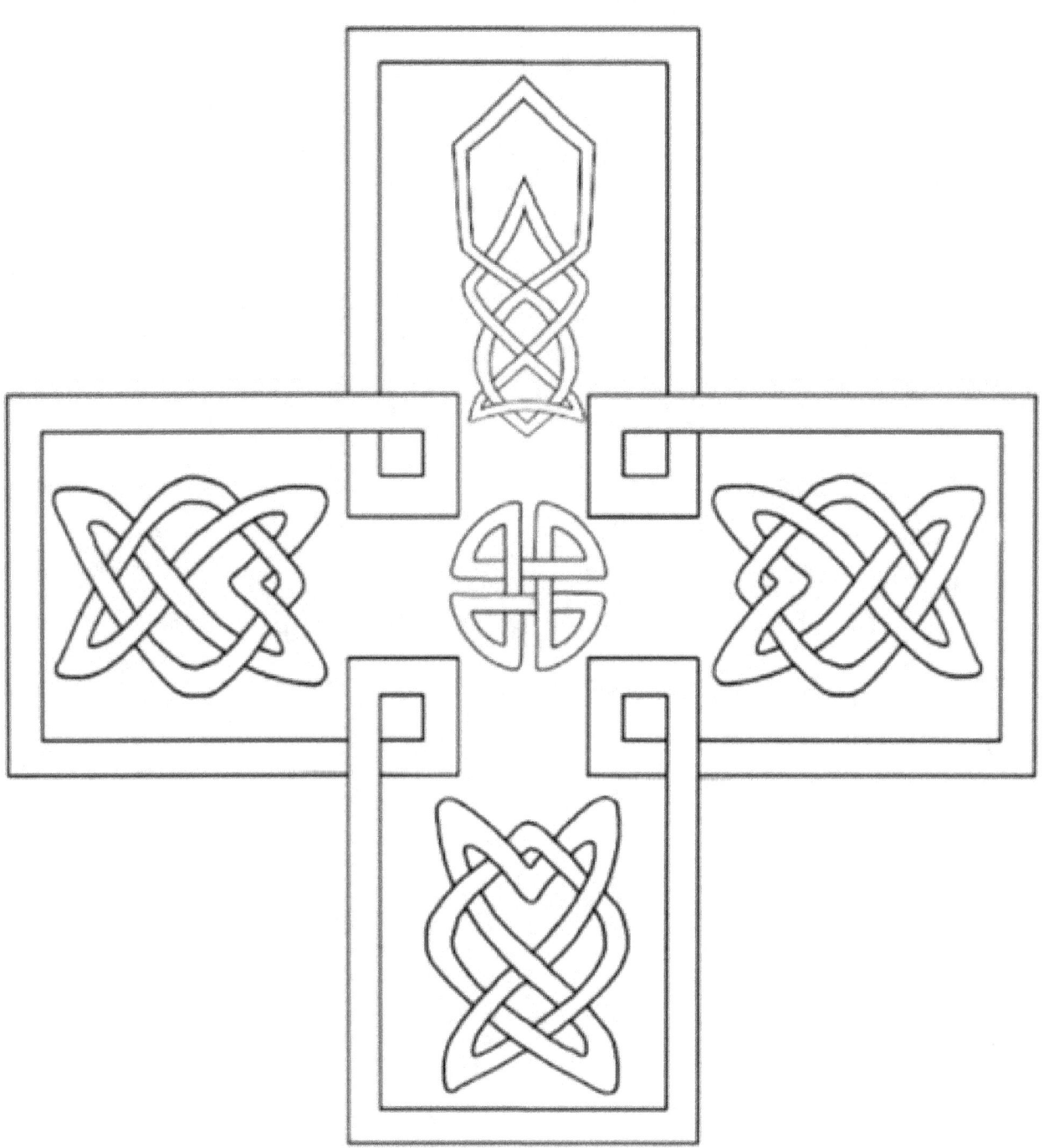

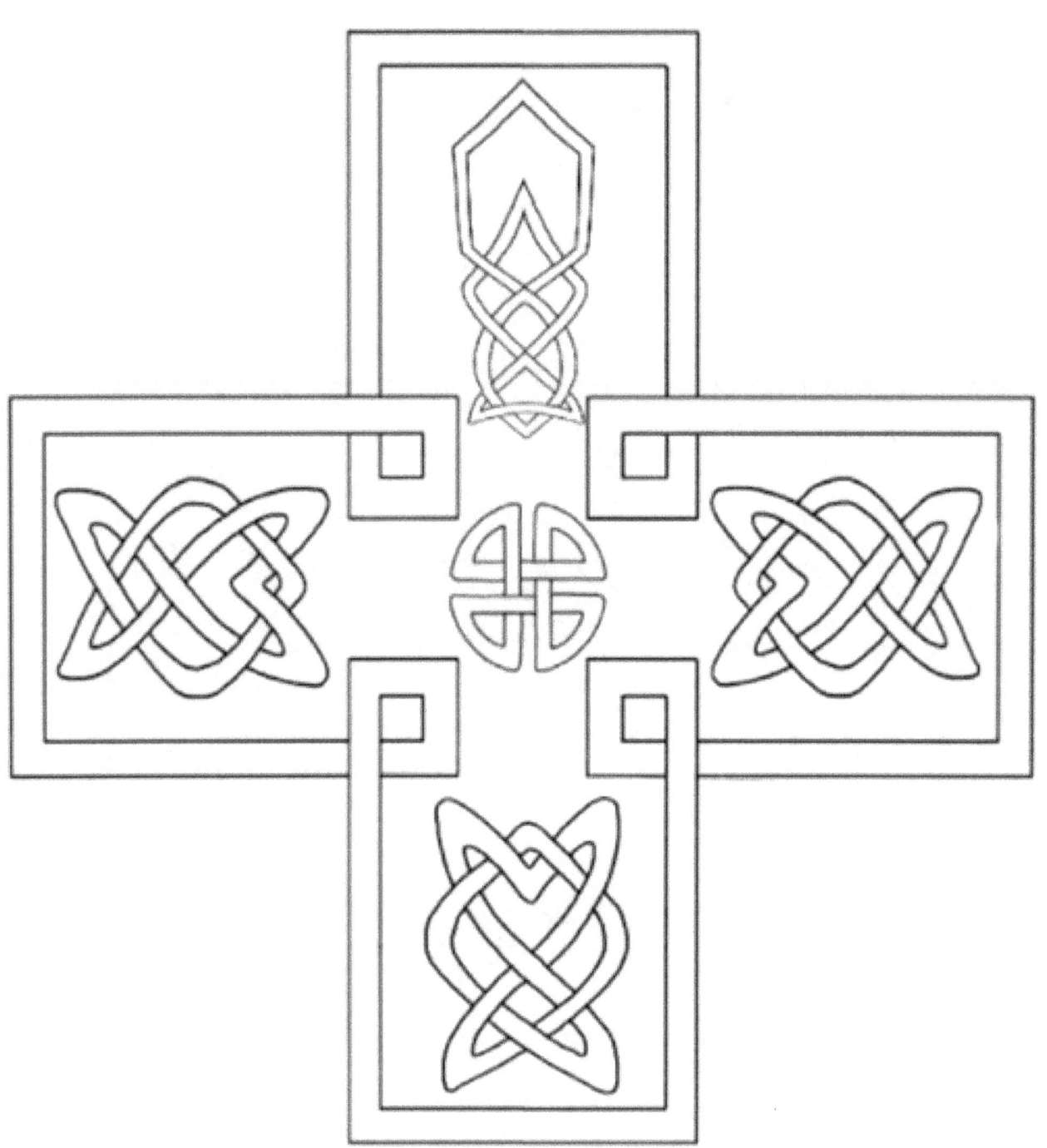

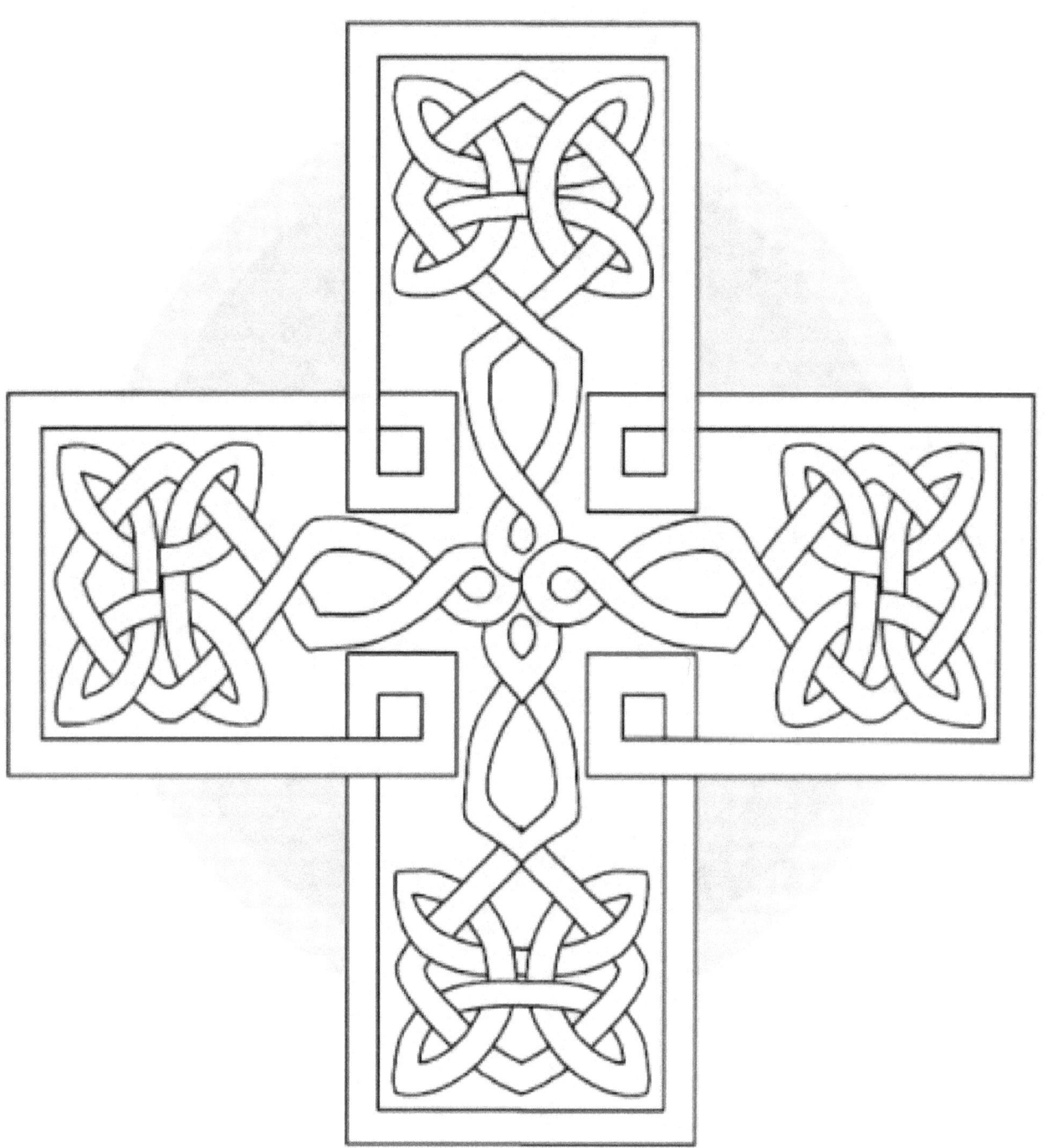

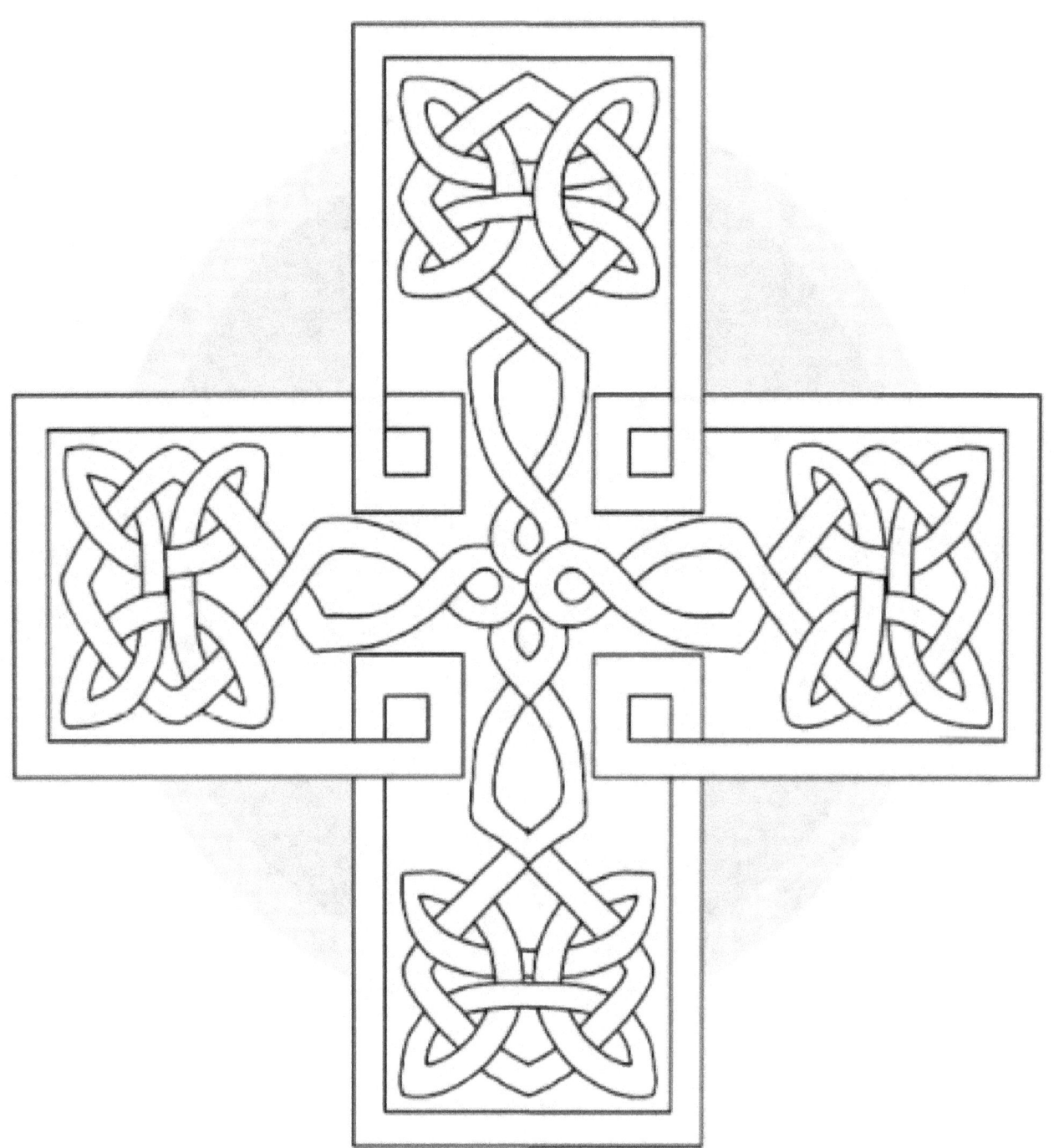

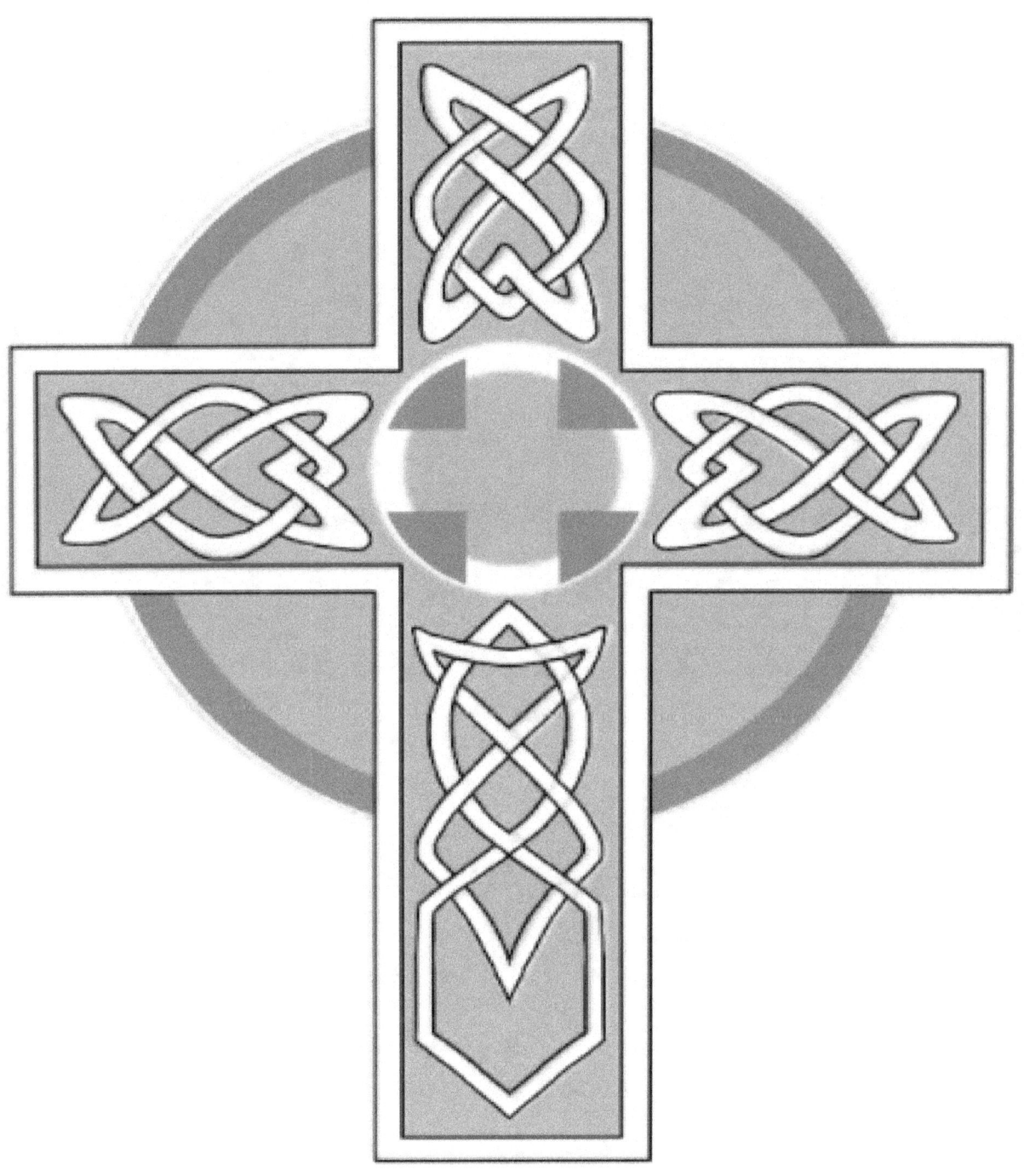

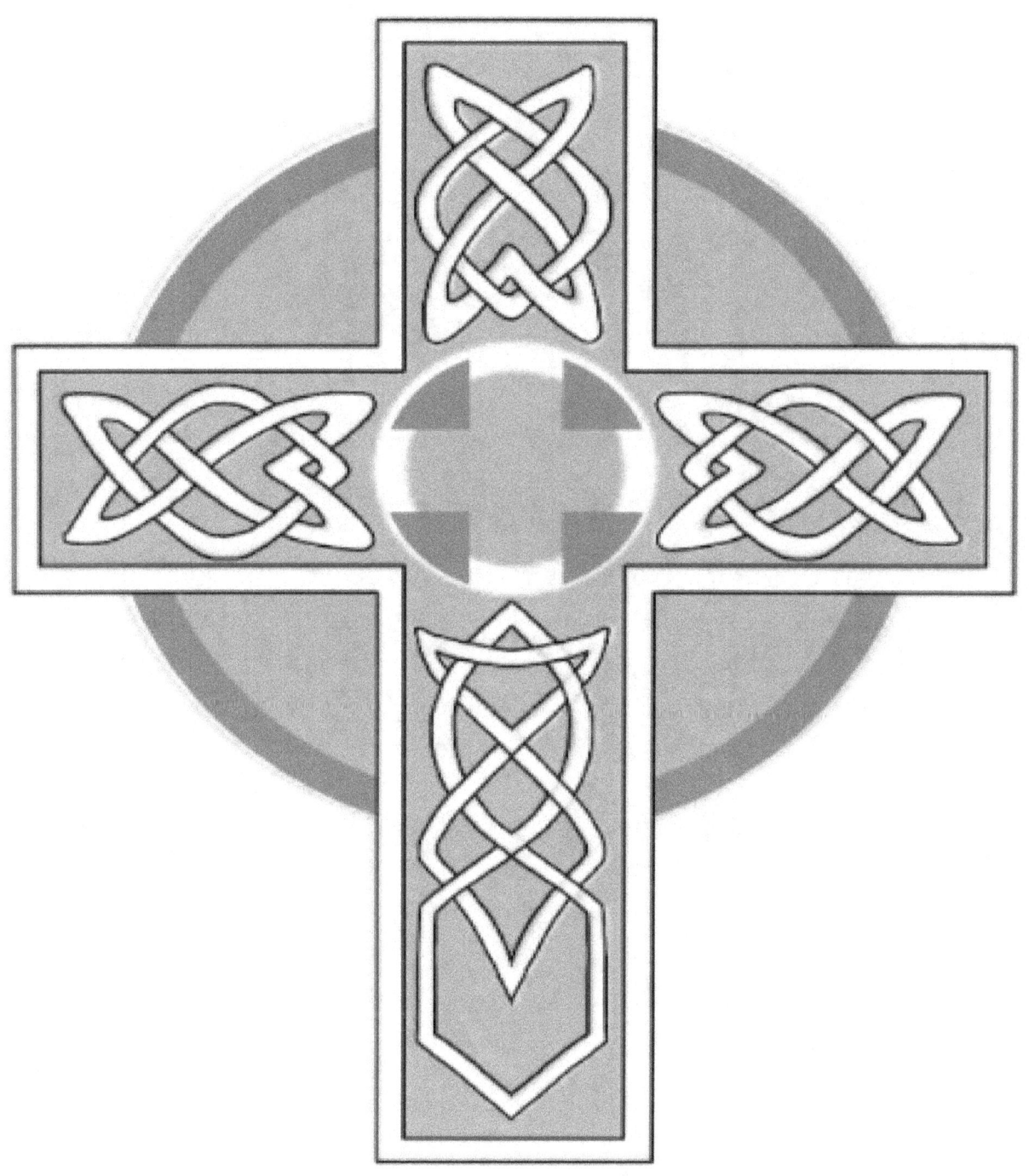

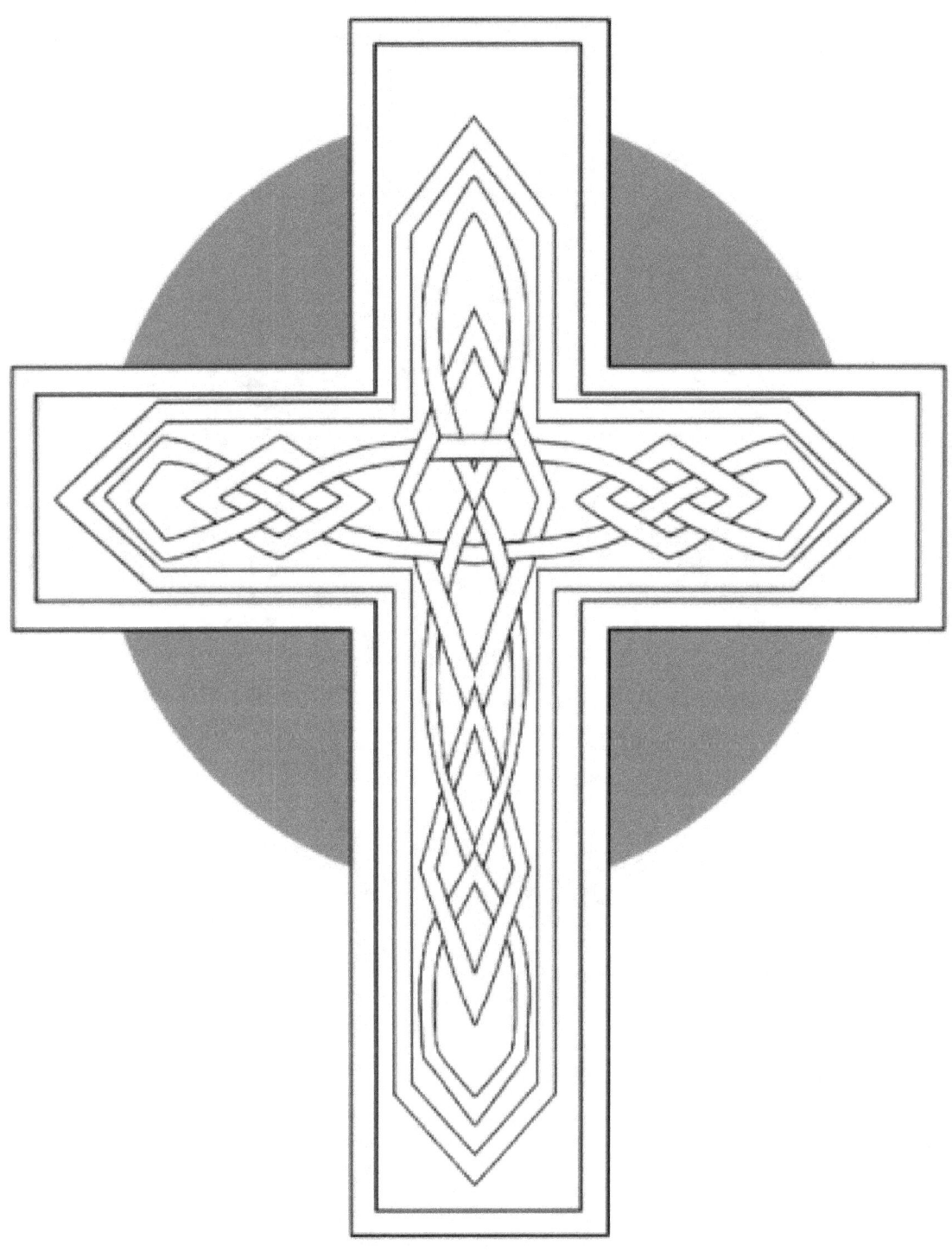

41

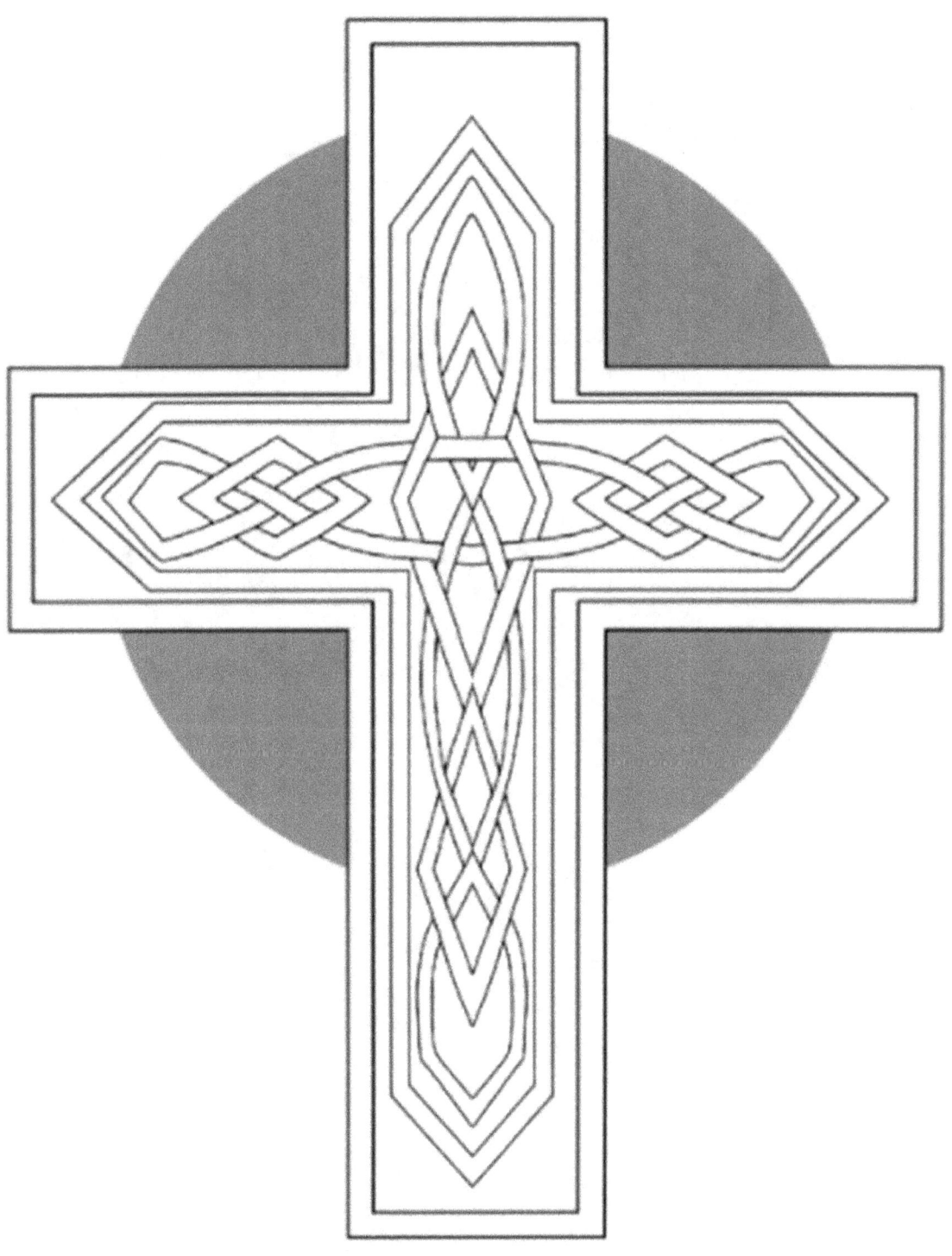

43

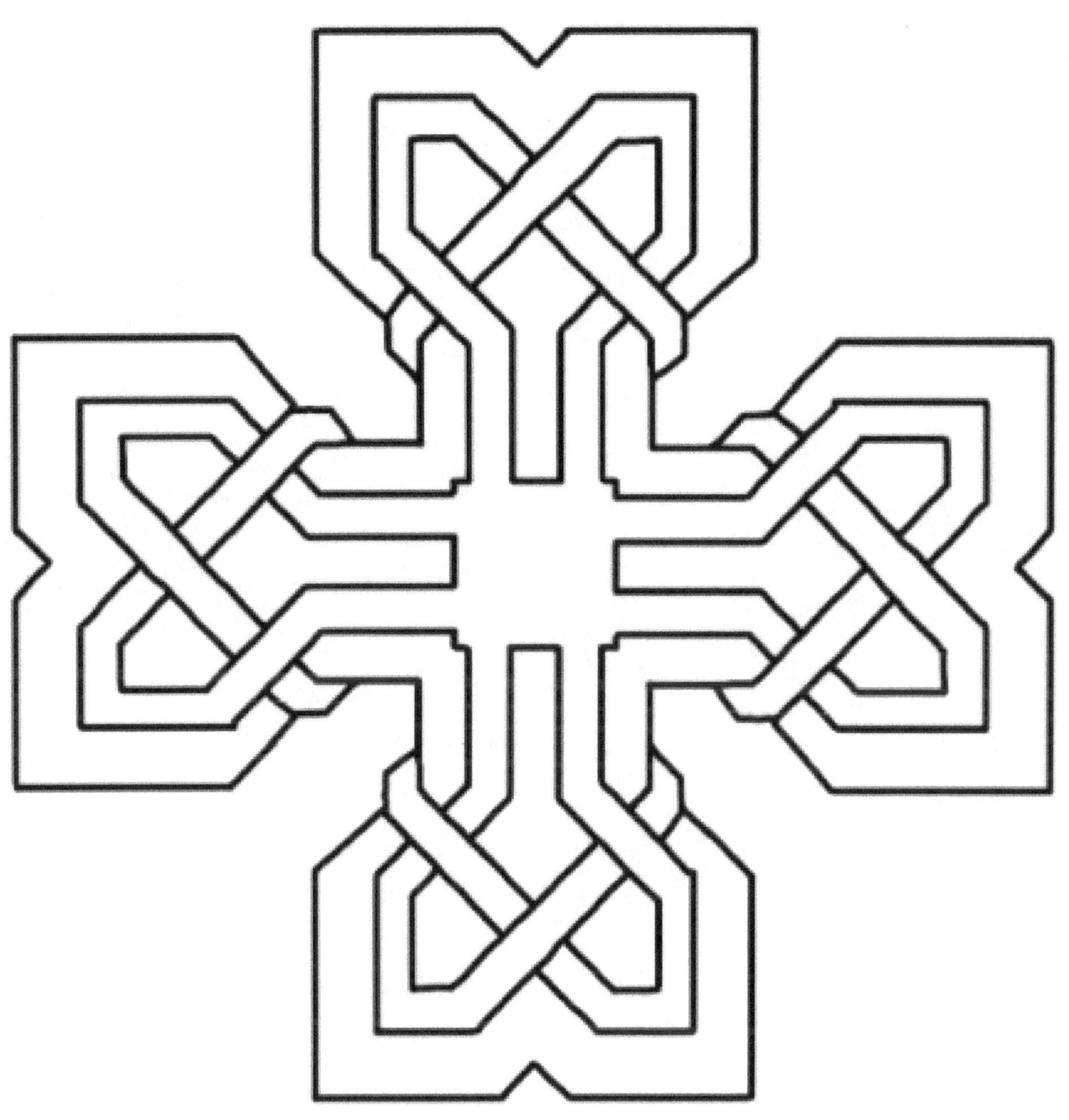

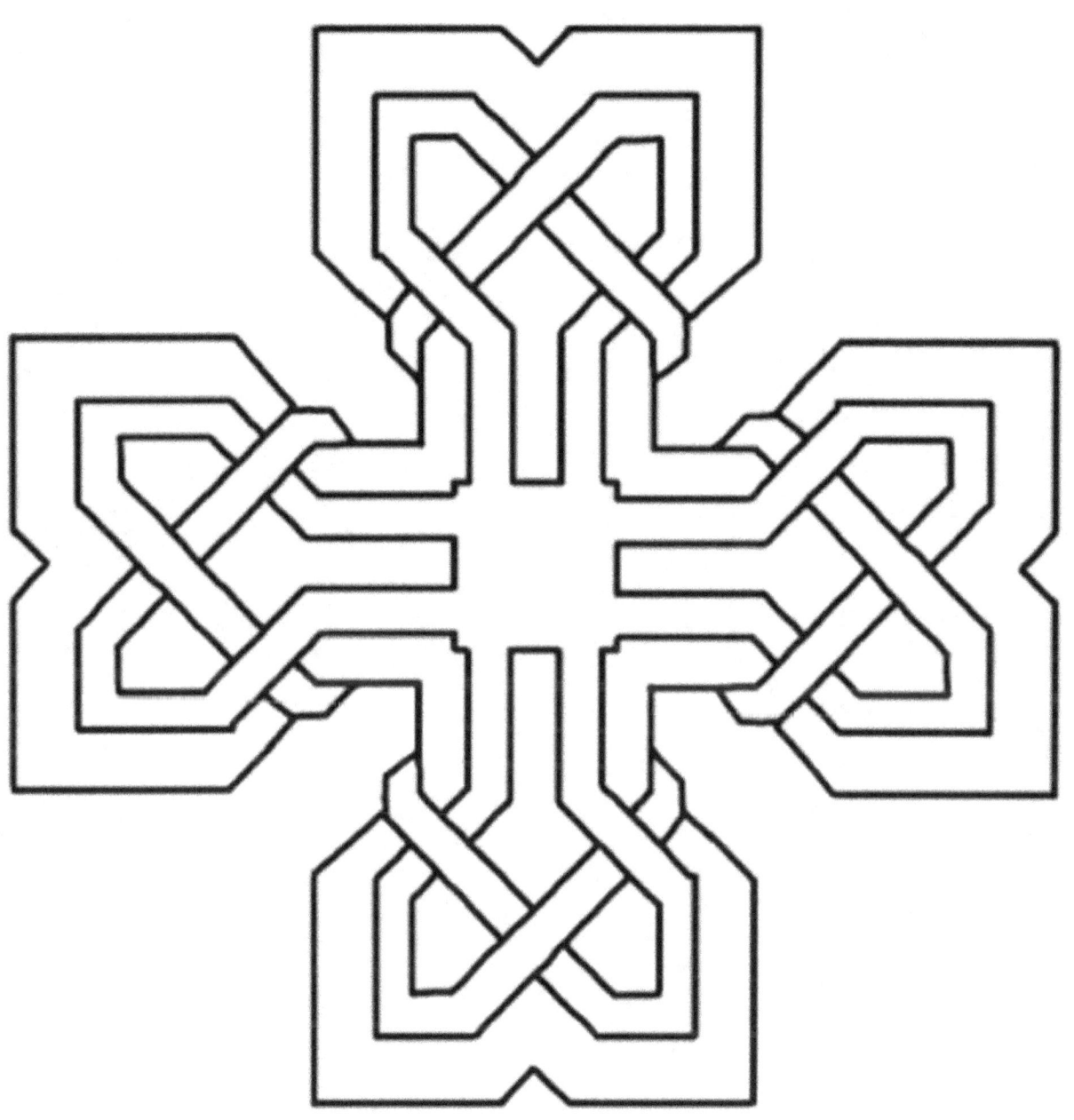

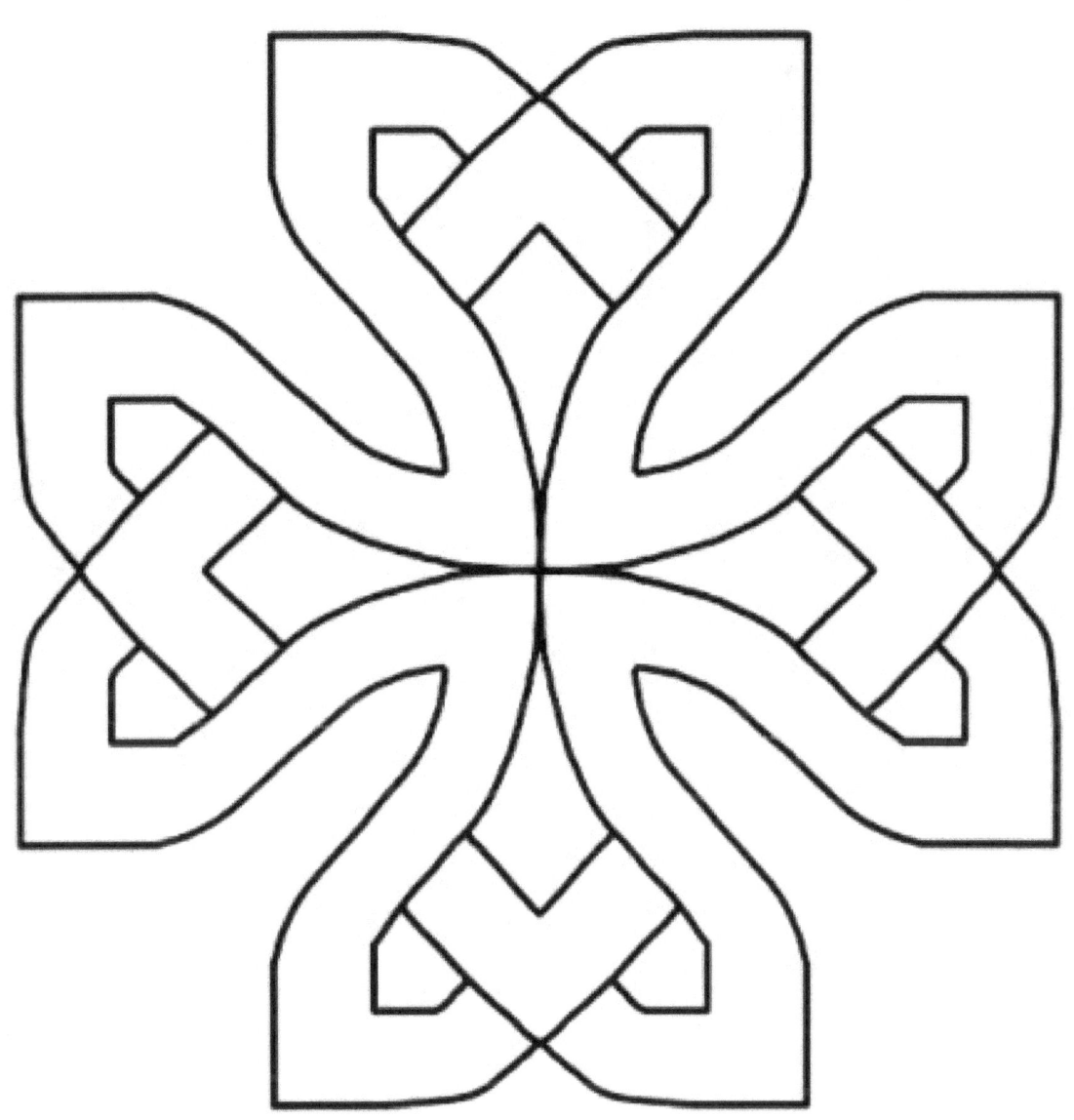

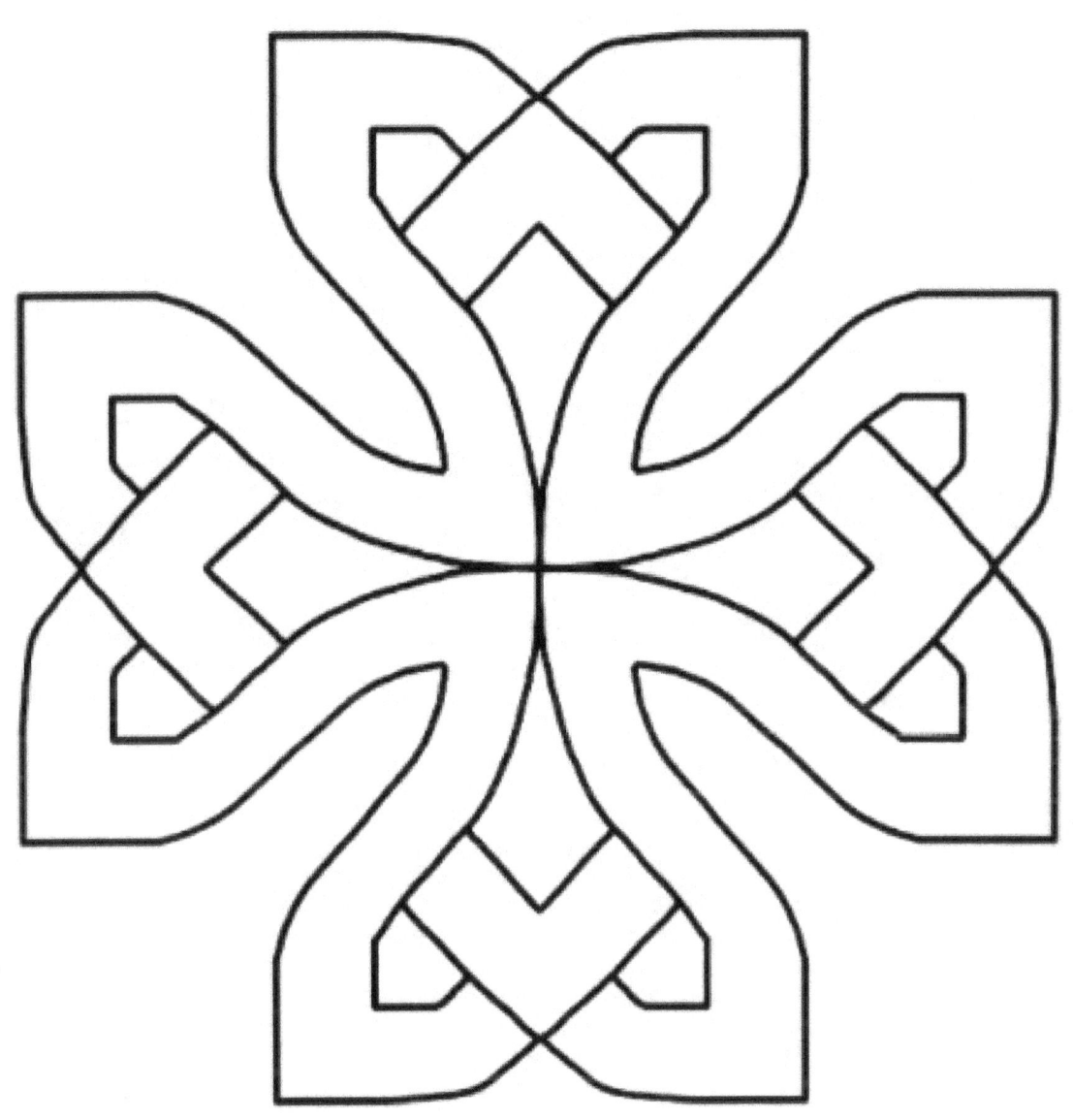

53

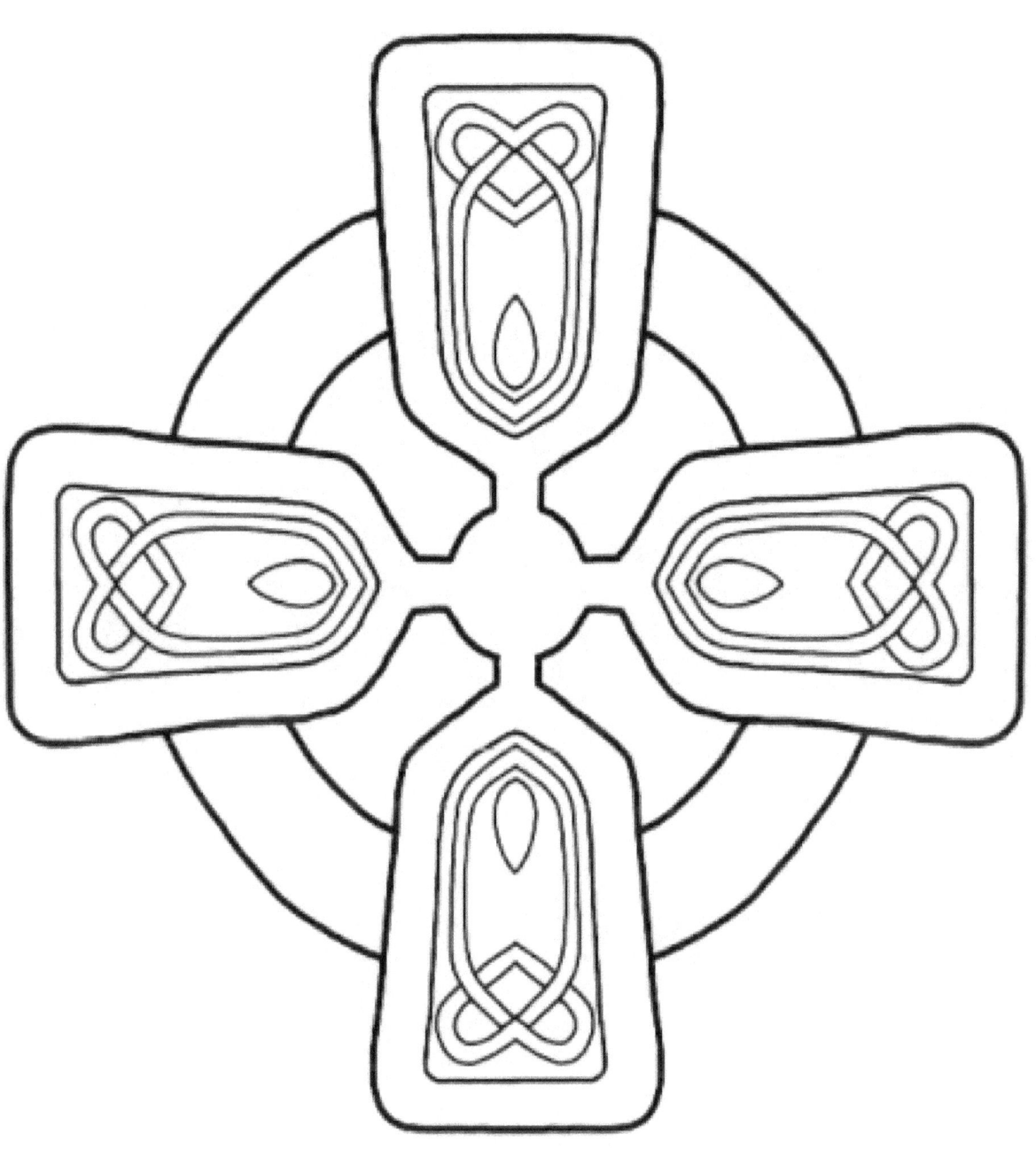

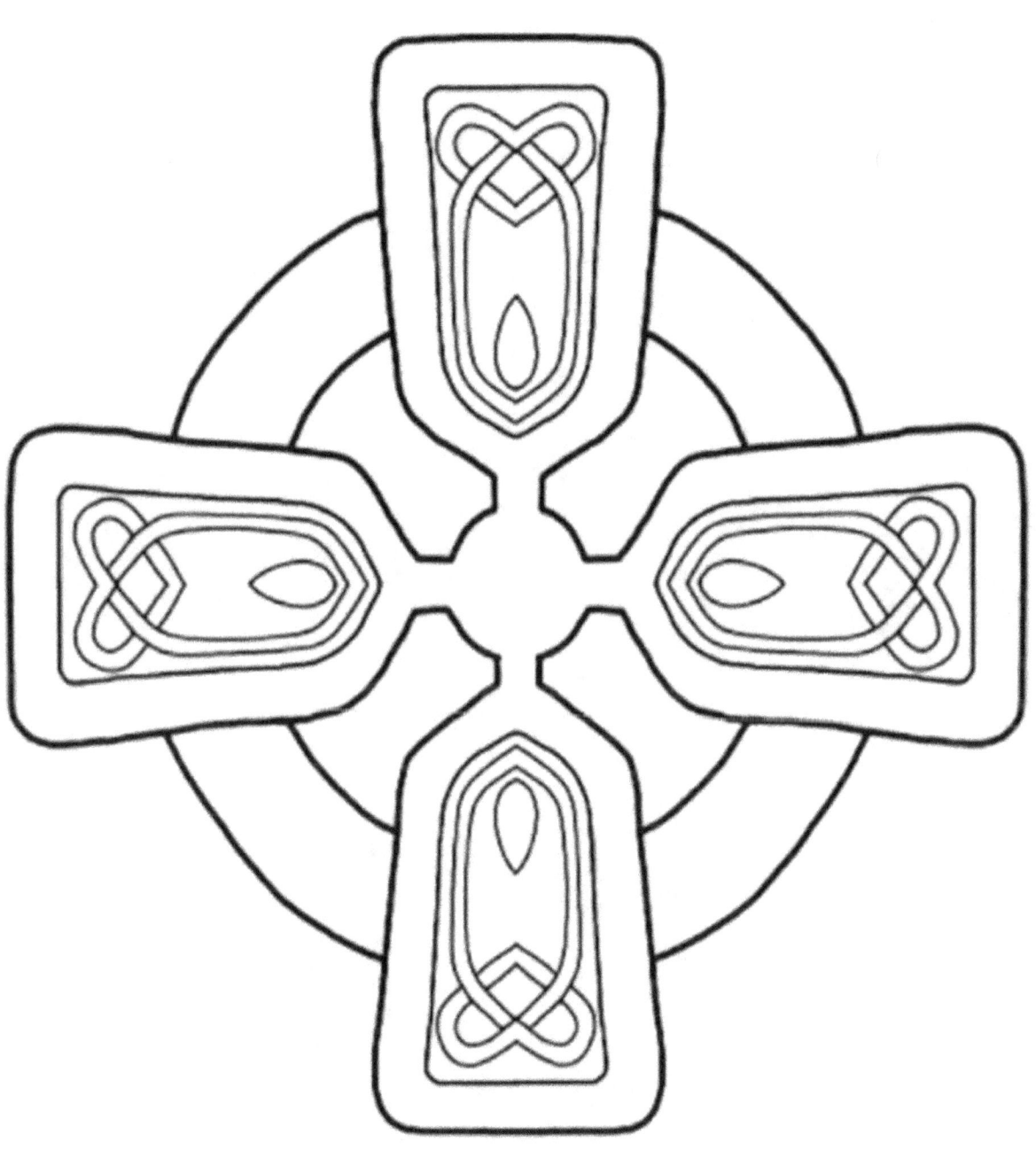

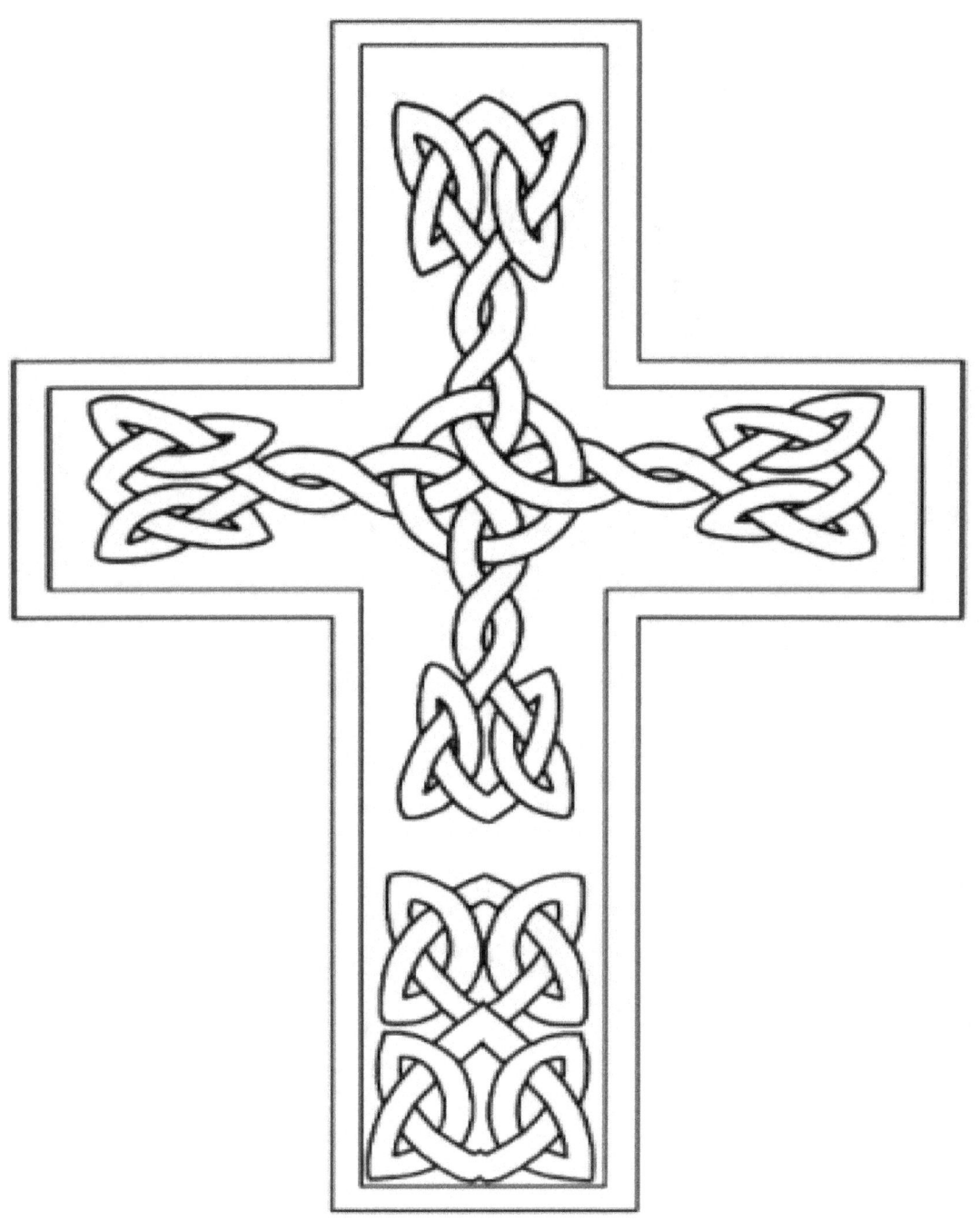

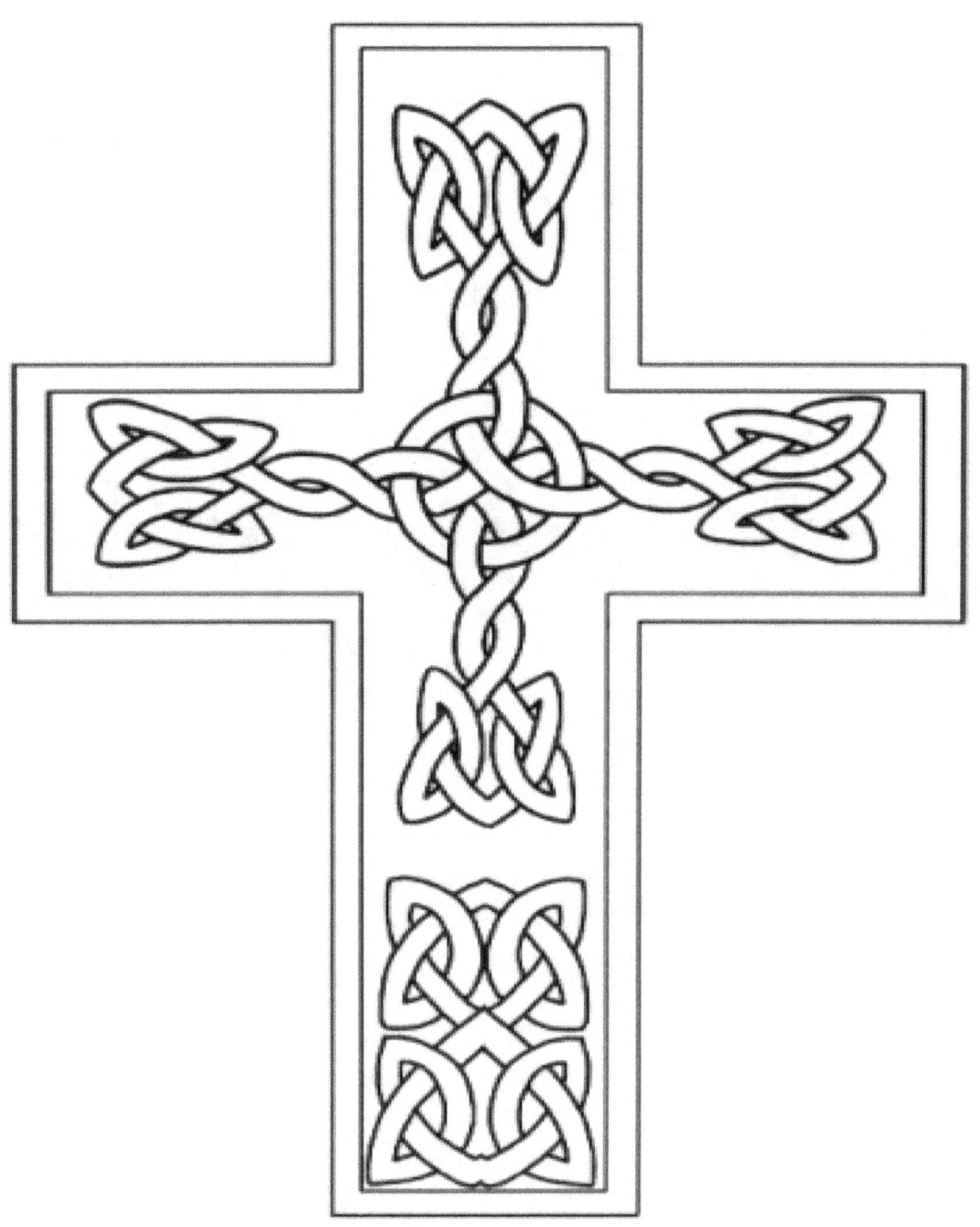

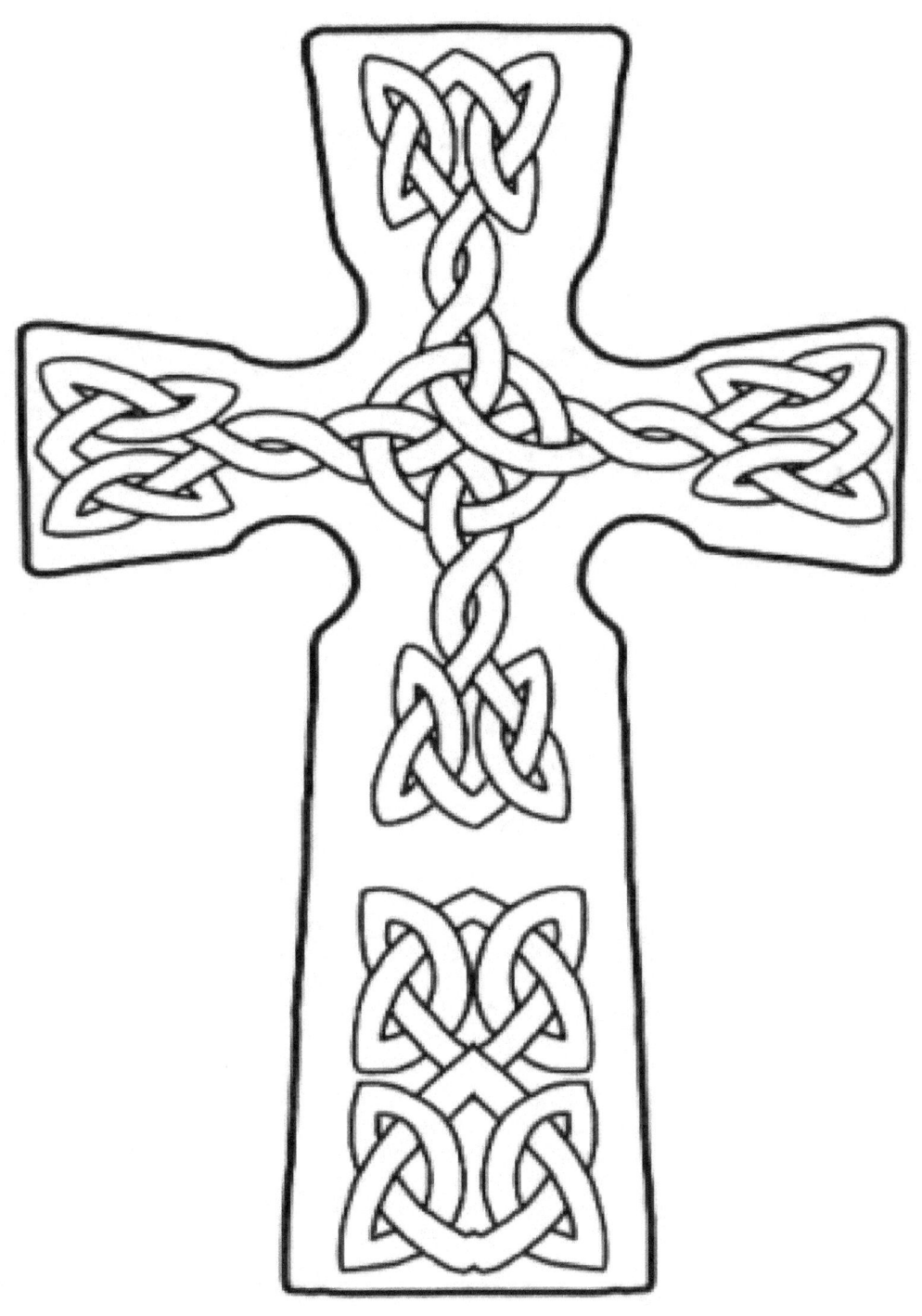

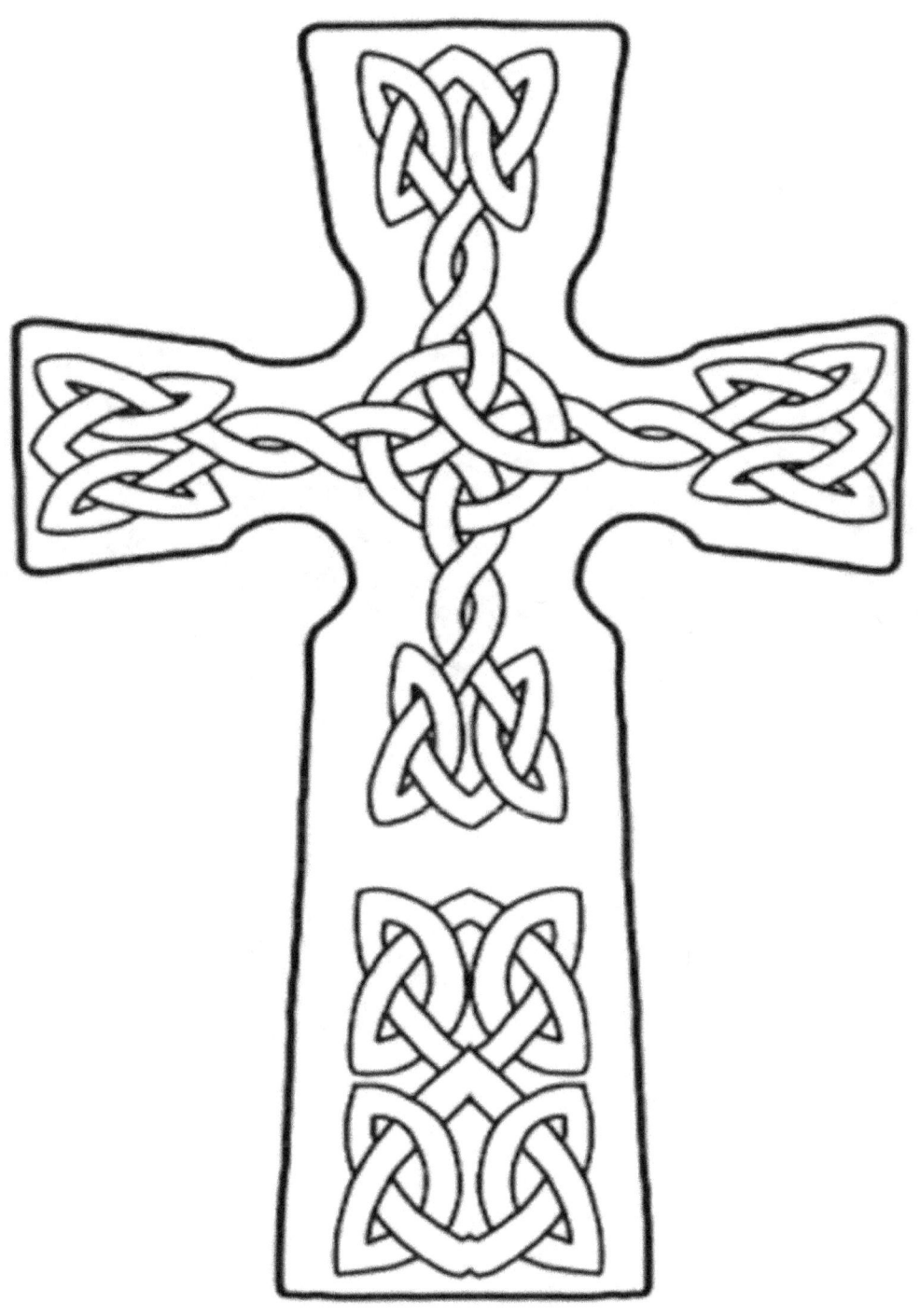

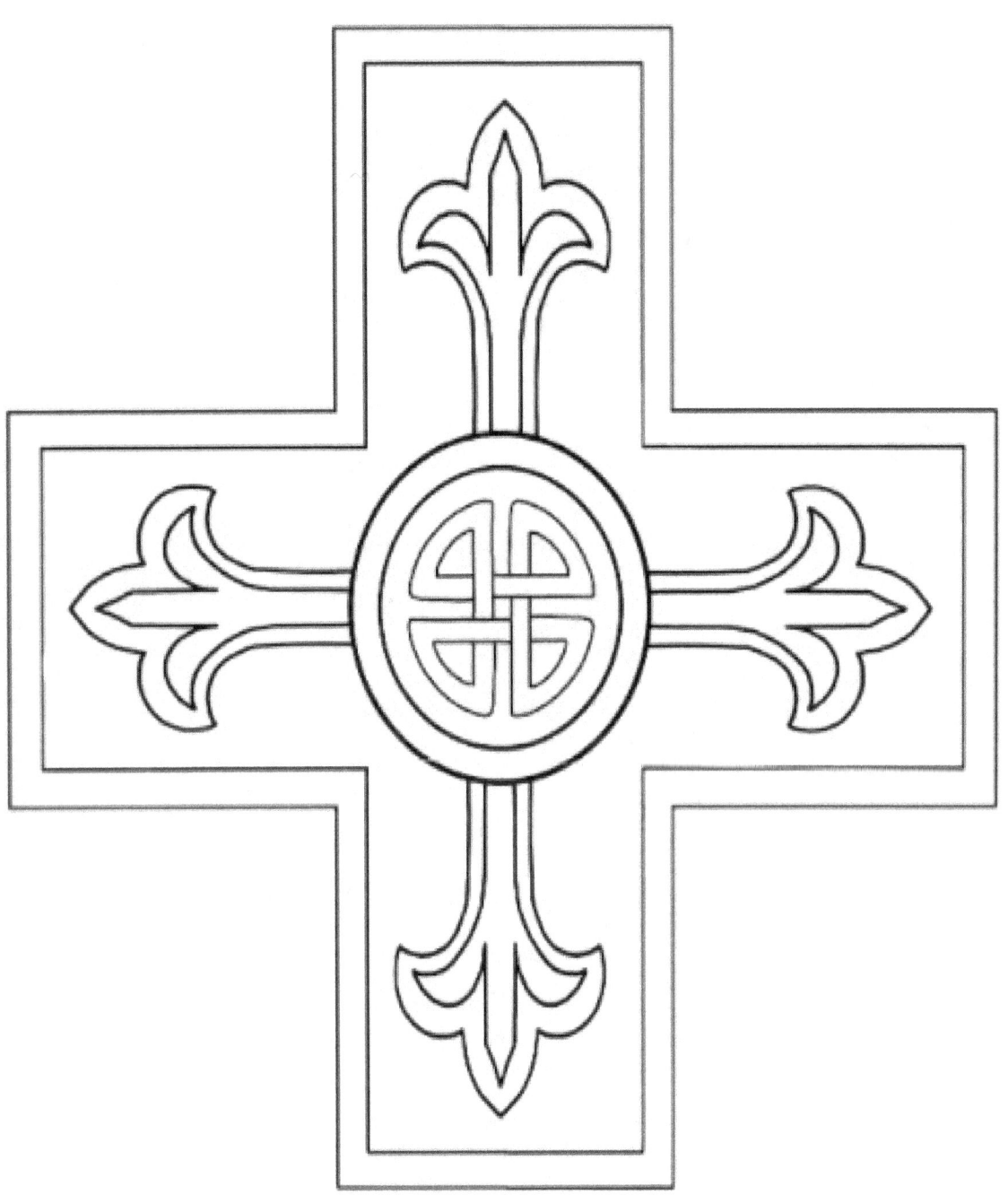

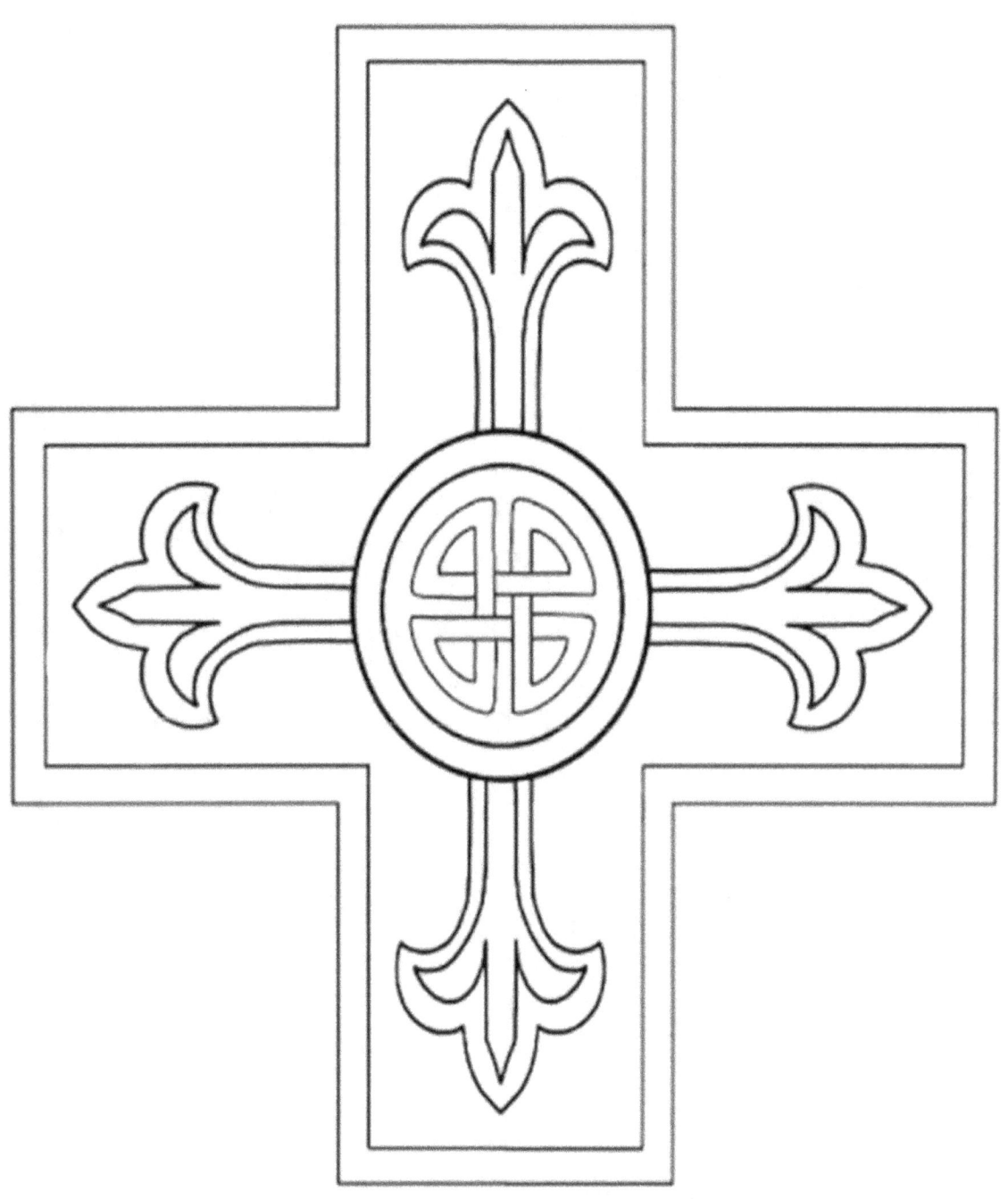

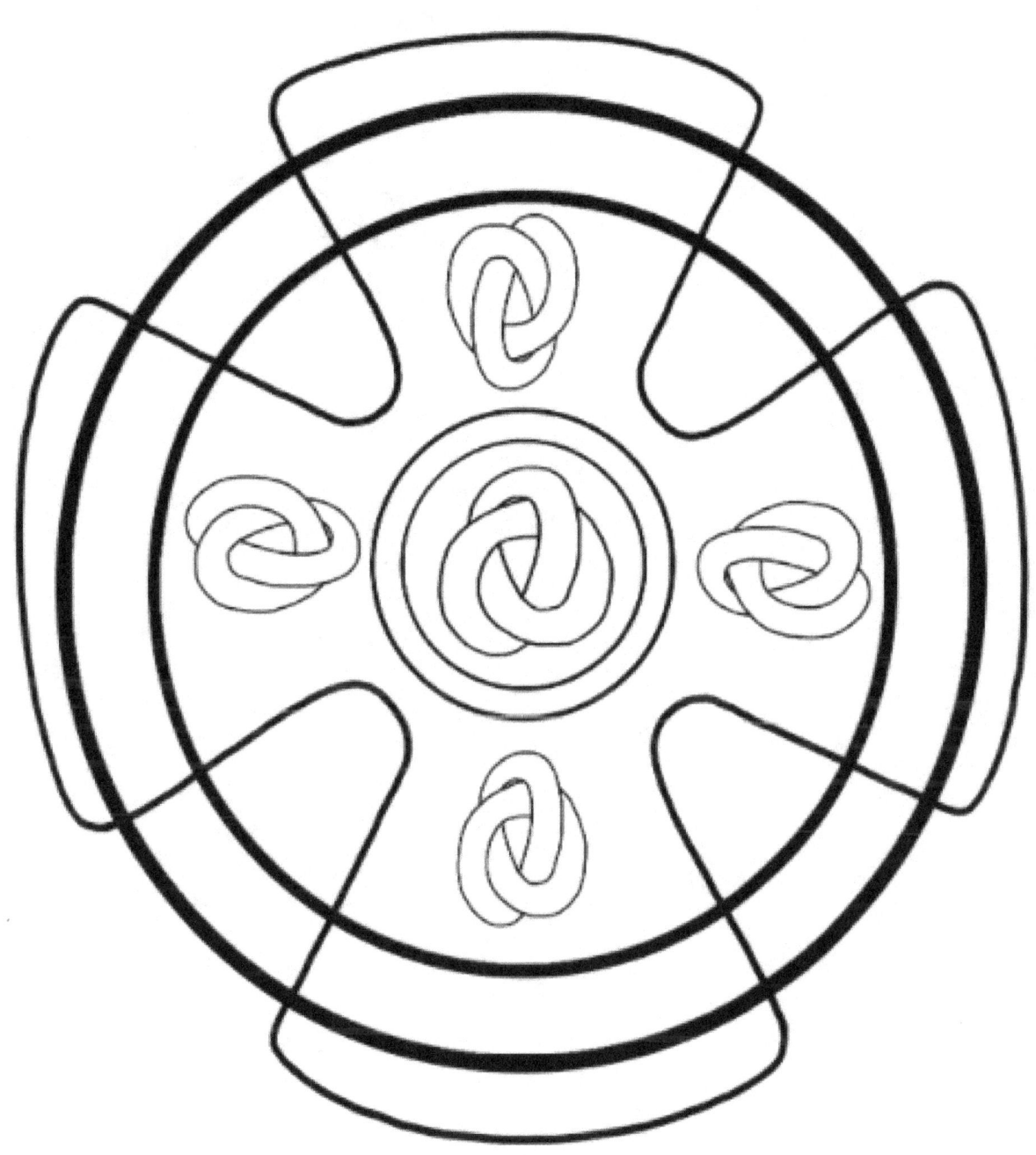

77

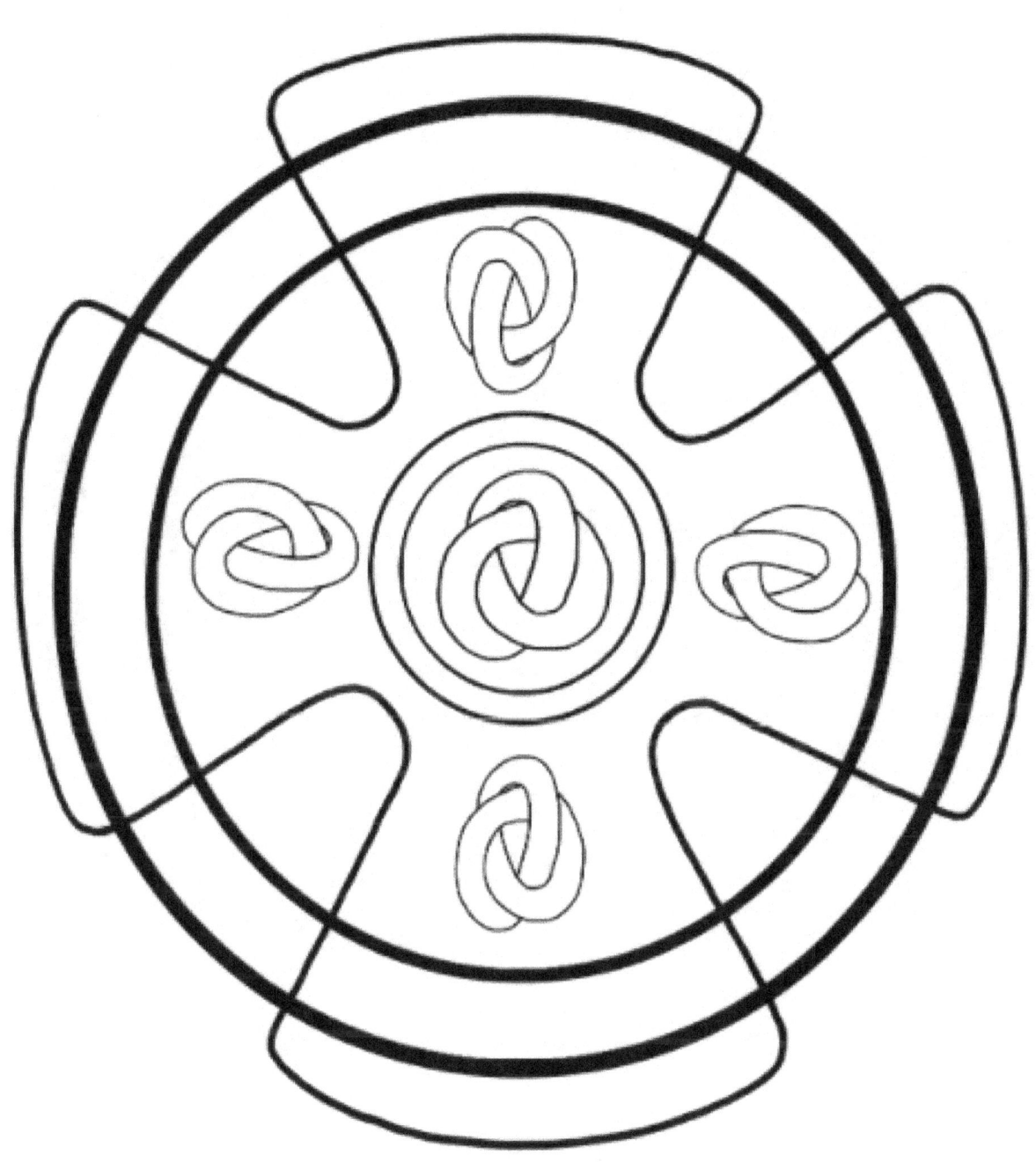

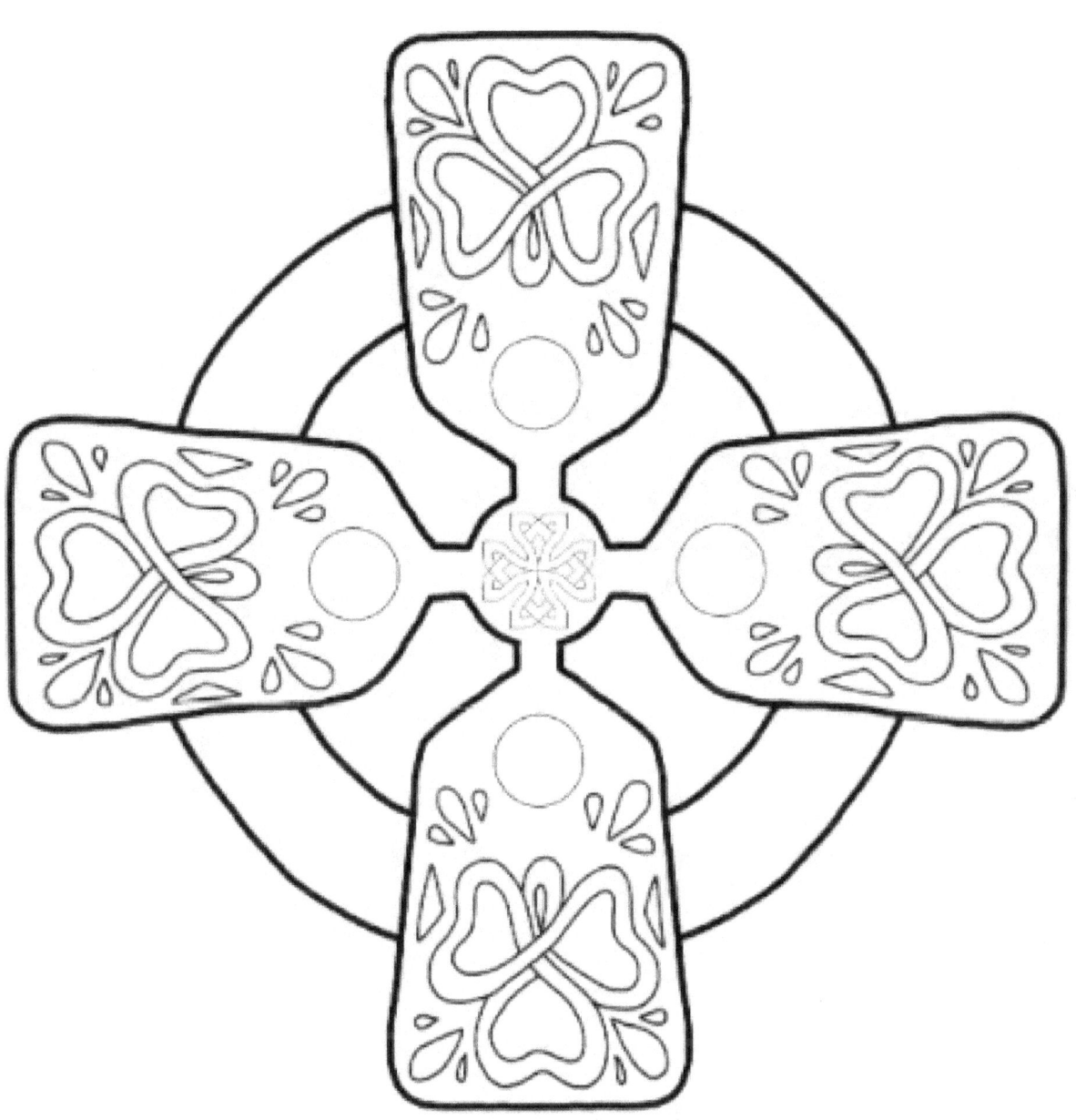

81

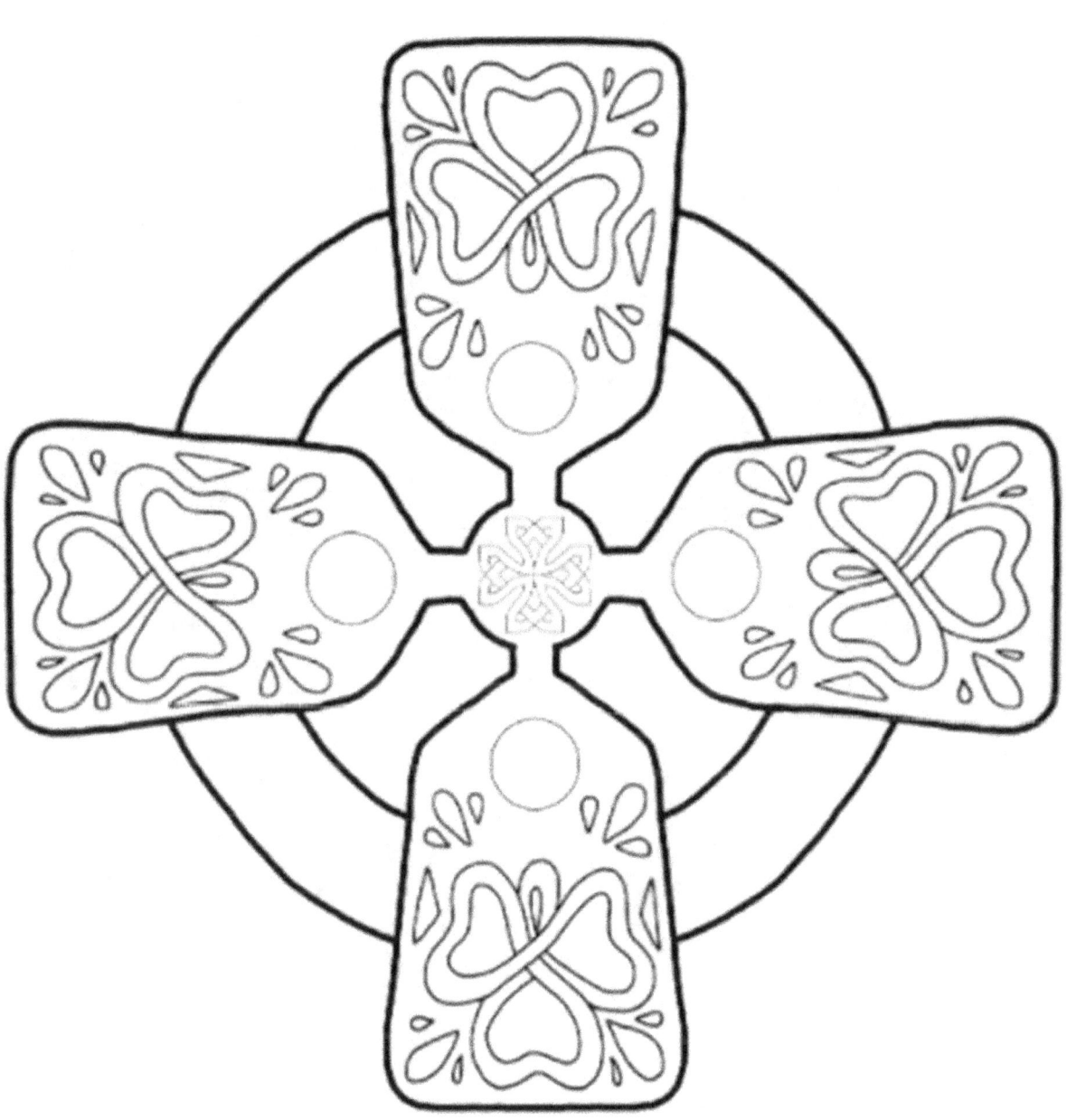

84

www.ingramcontent.com/pod-product-compliance
Lightning Source LLC
Chambersburg PA
CBHW080851220526

45467CB00008B/2469